SCM STUDYGUIDE TO THE OLD TESTAMENT

for Joshua David Barnett

gyda chariad

SCM STUDYGUIDE
TO THE
OLD TESTAMENT

John Holdsworth

scm press

© John Holdsworth 2005

British Library Cataloguing in Publication data

A catalogue record for this book is available
from the British Library

0 334 02985 6

First published in 2005 by SCM Press
9–17 St Albans Place, London N1 0NX

www.scm-canterburypress.co.uk

SCM Press is a division of
SCM-Canterbury Press Ltd

Printed and bound in Great Britain by
Biddles Ltd, www.biddles.co.uk

Contents

Acknowledgements

This book grew from the practice of teaching undergraduates and trainee ministers who did not expect to be swept off their feet by the Old Testament. I am grateful to those generations of students at Cardiff University, St Michaels Theological College and the South Wales Ordination Course who have encouraged me to define more clearly the wood and the trees. Among my colleagues, I am grateful for the support of Professor Stephen Pattison, and to Dr John Watt for his comments on work in progress. I have valued also the encouragement of Bishop Carl Cooper, the staff at SCM Press and, of course, my wife Sue. The coming to birth of the book has coincided with the coming to birth of our first grandchild who has both Jewish and Christian antecedents. It is both with a sense of appropriateness and great joy that I dedicate the book to him.

How to Use this Book

This book has been organized as a course. That is, it uses progression as a learning tool and assumes that those who read Chapter 7 will already have read Chapters 1 to 6. This is the same organizational principle as if you were learning a language – and so it is fairly important to work through it from the beginning. Having done that you will be able to refer intelligently to its parts, but this is not a biblical dictionary as such. Each chapter begins with a 'summary', that is: pages that will help you to access the subject of the chapter more fully. Each of these summaries introduces both the theme and the shape of the chapter. It gives references for the works cited and suggests what extra reading may be helpful. Generally, the second of these headings will be much fuller than the first, to avoid lots of off-putting reference material in the main text. Finally the summary will remind you of what you should know having completed the chapter.

Most of the chapters include two kinds of exercise. The first is a reflection on experience, which helps the reader to begin to reflect, from what is already known, about the general significance of the material to be studied. The second (of which there are generally two or three per session) is a reflection on text, which encourages the reader to use the text and to experiment with it in various ways, to gain confidence with it. The exercises are included as part of the course and should be done to gain maximum benefit. You may choose your own version of the text or even compare versions. Be aware of the main differences between versions. Some are translations, which try to stick closely to the original Hebrew. Others are paraphrases, which try to convey what the translator thinks the passage means. Others have an agenda (such as using gender-inclusive language) which identifies them as having approached the text in a particular way. Most scholars prefer as close a translation as possible. I generally use either the Revised Standard Version, the Revised English Bible or the New Jerusalem Bible.

Introduction

How to write an Introduction to an Introduction – That is the Question!

When I was in the third form at school we had an English teacher called Mr Jones. He it was who had the task of introducing me to the works of William Shakespeare. Perhaps that is why I am a theologian and not a Shakespearian scholar. For Mr Jones believed that the best way to introduce the bard to 13-year-olds was to encourage them to draw pictures of what the Globe Theatre might have looked like in Shakespeare's time. In the first place I couldn't draw, and in the second I was far more interested in whether to be or not to be, and how Romeo got off with Juliet. It is possible to write an introduction to the Old Testament that makes the same mistake. To those who want to know what relevance the Bible has to life nowadays and whether that affects me; or who want to learn more about God and faith and the other things religious people talk about, we offer lists of ancient kings and ground plans of Palestinian villages.

It was the same with French. My French textbook began with tables demonstrating how to conjugate verbs. After a year of learning whole series of seemingly unconnected similar kinds of skill I was still unable to string a sentence together or make any sense of a French menu. When I learned Welsh as a young adult it was a different story. I followed a television series which began with a very ordinary looking chap chatting up an extremely pretty girl with obvious success using such lines as 'I like coffee, do you like tea?' I decided on the spot that that was the language for me. It is possible to make that mistake with an Old Testament Introduction too. For readers who want to be able to work with the texts, to see coherence and theme and to make connections with the present practice of Christian communities we offer a piecemeal book-by-book approach littered with references to technical terms and famous theologians which looks about as interesting as the Leipzig telephone directory.

And here is the point. As one who also teaches and writes about communication, I believe that the first requirement of any piece of communication is that it must (a) be interesting and (b) have some regard to the listener's situation. That is equally true of a book about the Bible. The writer has to try to hear what the readers want. And yet for years scholars have been writing books which contain extremely erudite answers to questions no-one is asking. Hence this book begins with five chapters devoted to the Not-So-Frequently Asked Questions which I believe are crucial if anyone is going, not only to know about the Old Testament but actually to be interested in it.

The first-time student of the Old Testament is faced with something which at first sight is pretty bewildering. This 'book' is not so much a book as a library – and a library with quite obscure titles. What on earth is 'Deuteronomy' for example? In a competition for the world's most boring book title, surely 'Numbers' and '2 Chronicles' would at least be finalists. Who was Jeremiah and what was he lamenting about (whatever lamenting is)? And was there really someone called Zephaniah? Unlike most books we might pick up, there doesn't seem to be any kind of clue as to how we have to read it. What organizing principle has dictated that the collection assumes its present form, and how can we, the reader, get some kind of handle on it all? What, actually, is it *about*? A quick flick through will show that it contains some sections of poetry, some apparent descriptions of historical events, some reported speech of people who seem to be quite important, and whole sections of wise sayings, but it would be quite futile to launch into a description of the contents of these disparate items without answering questions like: Why was it written? Is there some key to the order of the books? Is it about what happened, or is the chief interest in the *interpretation* of what happened? Or is it meant to be read more like a series of stories, in which the question of whether what is described actually happened is irrelevant? How was it all put together and who did that and why? Above all, why do people still read this stuff as if it has relevance to today? What is it that Christian communities find here to give meaning to their lives and legitimacy to their actions, and how do they find it?

Exploring these questions will give us opportunity to see how scholars and other readers, through the centuries, have tried to make the Old Testament accessible. That in turn will give us the opportunity to see what options there are for us, as readers today, and help us to focus on what we aim to get from our reading and how realistic that is. The second part of the book will lead us through some of the writings that tell the story of Israel. It will also help us to reflect on the different perspectives which the biblical books present on the story of Israel, and to reflect on issues that are universal to humankind, and are recognizable to all of us. These are questions about why the world was created, what is my part in it, whether I have a destiny, why there is suffering, whether evil is stronger than goodness, and so on.

One important conclusion that readers should draw from the first part is that there are many ways of reading the Old Testament, and we haven't necessarily found the right one yet. This Introduction is not like the instructions for assembling a flat-pack wardrobe, in which there is only one correct route to a perfect product. This is more like instructions on how to use a hammer, in the full knowledge that some people think you must never use a hammer to build a wardrobe and that only a screwdriver will do. Nevertheless it will show you some of the products that have appeared, made with both hammers and screwdrivers, allowing you to see which you want in your bedroom. There has scarcely been a more interesting or exciting time to be studying the Old Testament. Historians of culture tell us that we live on the cusp of two ages: a 'modern' age and a 'postmodern' age and, as we shall see, that has huge repercussions for the ways we might study texts. New critical methods, to some extent connected to this movement between ages, have appeared and been developed during the past twenty years or so which have given some people a new sense of freedom and creativity as readers, and which have led to new ways of understanding theology. The task for today's readers is not simply to come along with an empty sack, to have it filled with a lot of expert knowledge from past ages; but rather to be real creative participants themselves in the theological task in more fluid theological communities.

I hope that this Introduction will convey something of that spirit of adventure and possibility. However, it will not neglect the questions which generations of readers have found useful, even if it approaches them from a different direction. After all, there are many people, I am sure, whose interest in Shakespeare was first kindled by drawing pictures of Jacobean theatres.

CHAPTER 1 SUMMARY

What is this chapter about?

This chapter sets a context for reading the Old Testament by briefly surveying trends in scholarship over the past hundred years or so. There is discussion about the differences between historically-based and literary-based methods of criticism, and an introduction to the tenets of practical theology.

What books are referred to?

The only book specifically referred to is W. Eichrodt, *Theology of the Old Testament*, trans. J. A. Baker (Philadelphia: Westminster Press, vol. 1 1961; vol. 2 1967). However, this is not a book to attempt at this stage.

What other books would be helpful?

Books which will be useful points of reference throughout the course include: J. Barton (ed.), *The Cambridge Companion to Biblical Interpretation* (Cambridge, Cambridge University Press, 1998) and James Barr, *The Concept of Biblical Theology: An Old Testament Perspective* (London: SCM Press, 1999), as well as other more basic Old Testament Introductions such as R. Coggins, *Introducing the Old Testament* (Oxford: Oxford University Press, 1990). An excellent companion for exploring the issues around the history of the Old Testament period is George Mendenhall, *Ancient Israel's Faith and History* (London: Westminster John Knox Press, 2001). A good introduction to issues of interpretation, once you've gained in confidence, is W. Brueggemann, *An Introduction to the Old Testament: The Canon and Christian Imagination* (London: Westminster John Knox Press, 2003). A selection of introductory books which have found favour during the last twenty-five years or so would include: J. Rogerson (ed.), *Beginning Old Testament Study* (London: SPCK, 1983); J. N. Schofield, *Law, Prophets and Writings* (London: SPCK, 1969); J. Barton, *Reading the Old Testament* (London: Darton, Longman & Todd, 1984); C. Westermann, *Handbook to the Old Testament* (London: SPCK, 1969); and R. Rendtorff, *The Old Testament: An Introduction* (London, SCM Press, 1985).

On literary methods of criticism in particular, the following reading list would be helpful:
David Gunn and Danna Fewell, *Narrative in the Hebrew Bible* (Oxford: Oxford University Press, 1993); The Bible and Culture Collective, *The Postmodern Bible* (New Haven: Yale University Press, 1995), Mark Allen Powell, *What is Narrative Criticism?* (London: SPCK, 1993); and A. K. M. Adam, *What is Post Modern Biblical Criticism?* (Minneapolis: Fortress Press, 1995).

How is the chapter organized?

The key topics dealt with are: what the title question means; how historically-based methods of criticism work; how literary-based methods of criticism work; what difference practical theological approaches make.

What should I be able to do by the end of this chapter?

Recognize current trends in critical study and their antecedents.

Distinguish between types of critical approach.

1

Why Read the Old Testament?

Usually, questions about *how* to do something are intimately tied up with questions about *why* it is being done. As a general rule that is also true of scholarship. The critical tools chosen are chosen precisely because they will yield the results that will best answer the questions the researcher is asking. With Old Testament scholarship, the last hundred years or so have seen an increasing frustration on the part of many scholars that the *how* questions and the *why* questions have become more and more separated. I remember speaking to an elderly clergyman about a beach mission in which he had been involved. He spoke with evident pride of the part he had played. 'At the beginning of the afternoon', he said, 'the children were all building sandcastles. But by the end of the afternoon they were building Palestinian houses.' I tried to look enthusiastic. But in truth I had my doubts that the organizers of the mission would have stated as one of their aims that children should know more about ancient building practice.

If you were to ask most people I know who have tried it, why they read the Old Testament, I think their replies might include variations on some of these themes.

- To learn more about God;
- To learn more about how faith communities tick;
- To learn more about life, its meaning and purpose; and so
- To know how to behave, what attitudes to adopt, what to strive for.

Reflection on experience

Think for a moment about why you want to read the Old Testament. Do any of the points above correspond to your aims? Do you have others you can add to the list? You might want to learn something that will inform views about how church life should be organized today, for example. How will you check, upon completing this book, whether it has done what you want it to do for you? You might like to jot down a few sentences beginning: 'When I have read this book I expect . . .' Keep the list and use it when you do reach the end to assess its success. If you are using the book in a group compare your expectations with others and see how many you have in common.

I doubt if many people would put 'I want to learn more about an ancient culture' at the top of the list, though it may be something you would like to know about in passing. It might seem perverse, then, that by the beginning of the twentieth century, scholars were concerned that the critical methods they were using were so failing to yield answers to the questions they were really asking that they felt constrained to start a completely new discipline called Old Testament theology to redress the balance. They were concerned that the methods adopted by scholars at that time had led to a lot of knowledge about little bits of the text, but very little about the big picture. They were concerned that there was a very full account available about religious ideas generally current in the ancient Near East, but very little attention paid to what was distinctive about Old Testament faith specifically. They feared that study to date was relatively superficial, lacking real engagement with the significance of what was described, nor having depth in meaning. They saw little contact with New Testament scholarship, or attempt to make meaningful links between the two Testaments that make up the Christian Bible. They accepted that quite a lot was known about religion in the sense of ritual and institutional practice but very little about how people understood or apprehended God in all this. A man called Walter Eichrodt was the first to try and address these concerns in a ground-breaking book called *Theology of the Old Testament*, first published in 1933. So how on earth did we get into this situation?

It's probably all down to the cultural movement we have already referred to called Modernism. Up until the Enlightenment, most people read the Old Testament primarily as a way of throwing more light on and providing a context for the New Testament. Ways of interpreting the text were relatively free and included *allegorical* and *typological* reading. An **allegory** is a story in which each of the parts of the story stands for something else. So for example, Song of Songs, which is an erotic love poem, was seen as an allegory in which the two lovers were actually Jesus and the church. Probably, it was because the book was seen in this way that it made it into the Old Testament at all. **Typology** sees models or types in the Old Testament that will reach their full presentation in the New. So the sacrifice of Isaac in Genesis 22 is seen as a type, a model, a forerunner of the real thing when God was content to see his son sacrificed on the cross, and so on. There are plenty of examples in the New Testament itself of reading the Old Testament in this way (see for example: Galatians 4.21—5.1; 1 Corinthians 10.1–11; John 3.14f.). With the advent of scientific thinking, led by Descartes and others, Christians began to feel like poor relations in the academic world. It was as if scientists had the real truth from the real world, testable by evidence and proof, and all Christians could offer were stories, allegories and fables. Scholars came to the defence of Christianity by trying to show that their truths, too, were open to rational enquiry and that Christianity was something more than a refuge for the ill-educated and ignorant. They wanted Bible study to hold its place in the academy. To do this they adopted the critical methods used by historians.

The so-called historical critical method of studying the Bible brought some new conditions and assumptions to the task. For historians and scientists, *objectivity* is a prime virtue. It is not enough that I think something. It has to be open to demonstrable proof such that anyone seeing the evidence will come to a common conclusion. For historians, *originality* is what is aimed for. With regard to texts, if I want to find out what a text really means I have to discover what it meant to those who first wrote it or those who first read and heard it. The task is to work back and try to uncover the layers of meaning which have overlaid a text over centuries, to get to that original meaning. There was, then, for those who followed this method, a real interest in how texts came to assume their current form. The assumption was that there is *one correct meaning* and one means of discovering it. Another assumption was that the text itself holds all the answers. It is *all-disclosing*. Current experience had no part to play in determining truth or meaning. It must be said that scholars saw this as an act of faith. This kind of enquiry, like science itself, was just one more way, they thought, of revealing God's great story, the plan of the creator. Religion had nothing to fear from science or academic investigation. A final consequence was that whereas until the Enlightenment the texts had been in the ownership, so to speak, of the church – it was the church that finally decided on matters of meaning in the texts – now a degree of ownership had been handed to the academics, albeit that they themselves were Christians. But the result was that in order to really appreciate the meaning of the texts you needed *experts*, people who could tell you what was originally meant because they had done the historical and textual research to enable them to do so. The ordinary reader was inadequate without them.

This development led to two kinds of tension, still discernible today. One was between the Christian academics and other academics who still looked with suspicion on religion. This came to a head on several occasions in the nineteenth century, largely to do with questions about evolution, and the method and date of creation. The other kind of tension was between Christian academics and the rest of the Christian community. Academics were increasingly accused of being out of touch with their base faith community. One response to this was a conservative backlash which would have nothing at all to do with academia or critical approaches and which opted for a kind of fundamentalism. With the benefit of hindsight one can have some sympathy with all sides of this debate.

Reflection on experience

How important is it, do you think, for reading the Old Testament, to have experts? And, if it is important, what kind of experts should they be? Come back to this question at the end of this chapter and see if your views have changed at all.

And so the kind of scholarship which was pursued with regard to the Old Testament, accompanied by new interest in archaeology, and discovering the facts from the desert sands, concentrated on how the texts were put together and transmitted, and what were the precise meanings of obscure Hebrew phrases. There was research into the possible routes taken during the Exodus, into the exact composition of religious rituals and festivals, and how what the Old Testament bore witness to was attested by other sources and other evidence of religious life in the ancient Near East among Israel's neighbours. Little by little the key indicator of success came to be proving that what the Bible described really did happen, or, somewhat later, that it did conform to patterns discernible in the religious life of the area. So we arrived at the situation which made Eichrodt and others so anxious. The early twentieth century saw sterling attempts to address his concerns while still adhering to the general rules and assumptions of the historical critical method.

It is important to stress that not all this work had a negative result. Even those who in more recent times have adopted different methods of reading, acknowledge their debt to it. The work does help us to understand how the books of the Bible were formed and it helps us to appreciate the contexts from which it derived. It has rescued the Bible, and the Old Testament in particular, from being seen in a superstitious way as unrelated to real people and events, somehow just dictated from heaven. It has helped us to a more sophisticated understanding of the role of ritual and symbol, very important in the Old Testament, and to see the people of Old Testament times as, in a sense, people like us. It has denied any interpretation of the texts that sees them as a simple textbook for life, like the Highway Code, which can easily be understood and applied as a ready reference in all modern situations. The writings were designed for specific times, situations and cultures, and their authors had no awareness that they were contributing to Holy Writ or that they would be read in a completely different culture thousands of miles away and thousands of years in the future. I find salutary the story of the man whose reason for reading the Bible was to gain guidance in situations of perplexity, and who believed it could be read without any critical under-standing at all. His method was simply to open the book at random and run his finger down the page until he felt called to stop. When one such situation arose he followed this pattern and read 'And Judas went and hanged him-self.' Thinking this was a strange response to his predicament he tried again, and read, 'Go thou and do likewise.'

By the end of the twentieth century, the Modern era was drawing to its close. Western society no longer believed that there was one big truth, one big story, to be discovered or to be part of. The cry was now: 'You show me your truth and I'll show you mine.' This cultural move coincided with a new move in biblical criticism. Instead of examining the Bible using the insights and methods of historians, there was a new move to examine it using the methods and insights used by students of literature.

Reflection on experience

What do you think might be the differences for you between reading an historical document using the methods outlined above and reading an historical novel or a Shakespeare history play? Think about:

- what you need to know in order to appreciate the work
- whether you need expertise
- whether 'what really happened' is important
- the things that would most interest you in studying the novel or play
- how you would decide what the message of the work was and whether it was important to you.

For literary scholars there is not just one meaning but lots of them, and effectively the reader decides where the truth lies, though it may still be important to see how the writer's art is employed to persuade you of one truth rather than another. With this approach, originality is not the key thing because a truly great work of literature may have layers of meaning to subsequent generations which were not dreamt of by the original author. Subjectivity rather than objectivity is important. If I am moved by a passage that leaves you cold it does not mean that one of us is right and another wrong. There is little interest in how the work was researched or how it reached its final form. And importantly, culturally, you no longer *need* experts, useful though they may be in some circumstances. Proponents of these approaches would claim therefore that the text was freed from either scholarly or ecclesiastical control. We shall examine some of the repercussions of this in subsequent chapters, but in general this has led to a whole new critical enterprise with regard to the Old Testament, where most of what is said about God is contained in narratives or stories.

Literary criticism

The term 'literary criticism' is used by different scholars in different ways. Rather confusingly the term can be used to describe some aspects of historical criticism! Those scholars who want to claim that the critical methods appropriate for a study of literature are preferable to those employed by historians speak about:

* *Narrative*: they analyse character and plot, and are particularly interested in those parts of the Old Testament which are written in story form;
* *Rhetoric*: they analyse the literary devices a writer uses to persuade us of a particular point of view;
* *Reader-response*: they analyse the text by reading into it rather than reading out of it: by **eisegesis** rather than **exegesis**, whose chief interest is in the effect the text has on us, and the connections we make as a result of reading it;
* *Structure*: they look for patterns in the writing which are universal to all literature and allow links to be made with anthropological studies about how people communicate ideas, and with how languages have developed.

This kind of critical approach is still at an early stage but many would claim that as a method it stands a better chance of answering Eichrodt's anxieties than does historical method. A basic problem is that it ignores the question 'What really happened?' which many Christians believe is to some degree important in their faith. The method was, after all, devised to study fiction. Also, as a reaction to historical method it runs the risk of throwing out the baby with the bathwater. Even if we come to regard the Bible more and more as a literary work we shall still be interested in the question about what kind of people wanted to tell their story in this way or what kind of experiences informed and prompted their storytelling. We might also develop more of an interest in how different readers have understood it through the ages (what scholars call reception history). One of the things we shall see about the Old Testament itself is that it bears witness to the fact that different generations of readers in ancient times reinterpreted their ancient traditions in different ways to enable them to speak to their own generation. It is probably best to keep an open mind and allow our questions to be informed by both ways of reading the text.

It could well be that, like me, your reasons for and expectations about reading the Old Testament owe something to ideas about how the Bible should be used by the Christian community. In other words they could be part of a response to the question, what is the function of the Bible in the church? Throughout the ages and even today some people use the Bible on a verse-by-verse basis to argue about some issue of modern morality or church practice. I believe this is an abuse of the Bible which usually ignores its context and genre. I also believe that this is not how debate about morality or church practice should be conducted either. Similarly, the Bible has often been used to build and formulate doctrines of the church. This is not wrong in itself, but modern trends in theology, and especially thinking about the church, within theology, have taken a different direction which gives the Bible a different role.

The last thirty years or so have seen the growth of Practical Theology (sometimes called Pastoral or Applied Theology). This is a way of doing theology which it is claimed is appropriate in a postmodern age. The basic claim is that theology does not consist solely of propositions about God which have to be signed up to. Rather theology *happens* when Christian tradition comes face to face with experience, in a context of reflection. The church provides such a context. The process of reflection itself should enable a kind of conversation between Christian tradition and a given context such that each of those can be potentially transformed by the encounter. It works like this. I read the Bible. That gives me a new insight which I want to apply to the place where I live or work or care about. The title 'Pastoral Theology' suggests that these situations will often be ones in which questions about appropriate pastoral care are raised. Hence this will have a particular resonance with all for whom the category 'ministry' is important in some way. The change that is brought about in the situation provides me with a new insight as to the meaning of the text. And so the cycle begins again. Clearly the Bible has a crucial role in such a process.

And so I want to read the Old Testament in a way that will be *useful* in that enterprise. I want to read something that potentially will capture my imagination, and potentially transform my understanding, situation and world. I do not want to read out of idle interest or in a way which protects me from the challenges which the word of God should always present. And that means taking a special interest in why the writers wrote. Were they simple recorders, or were they too, theologians – people who wanted to make sense of their world and predicaments by reflecting again on the ancient stories about God? If they are to enter my world, I need to enter theirs – and that means something more than building sandcastles.

CHAPTER 2 SUMMARY

What is this chapter about?

This chapter builds on the insights gained in Chapter 1 to explore further questions about reading related to those about the composition of the Old Testament.

What books are referred to?

The only new work referred to is Douglas Stewart, *Exegesis: A Handbook for Students and Pastors*, 3rd edn (Louisville: Westminster John Knox Press, 2001).

What other books would be helpful?

The books referred to in Chapter 1 will all deal with the questions raised here. A further book which helps de-mystify the biblical-critical process is Michael Joseph Brown, *What They Don't Tell You: A Survivor's Guide to Biblical Studies* (Louisville: Westminster John Knox Press, 2000).

How is the chapter organized?

The chapter investigates the following topics: Common misconceptions about the Bible; Inspiration; Source criticism, Exegesis; the Documentary Hypothesis.

What should I be able to do by the end of this chapter?

Describe what is meant by the terms exegesis, inspiration, source criticism.

Illustrate the method of source criticism with reference to specific texts.

2

Why Did the Writers Write?

The second of our QOAFA (Questions that Ought to be Asked Frequently but Aren't) is about the authors of the Old Testament. Usually, questions about authorship are quite important in written works. Given that we've already discovered that the Old Testament is more like a library than a book, imagine the following scene. The Reader goes into the Old Testament Library and speaks to the Librarian.

Librarian: How did you get on with Deuteronomy?
Reader: Oh, I really enjoyed it. Have you anything else by the same author?
Librarian: Well actually it's part of a series and the next one in the sequence is Joshua, but it's out at the moment.
Reader: Do you have anything else at all?
Librarian: Well to be honest, quite a lot of people skip through the series. The most popular book, probably because of the sex scenes, is 2 Samuel, but if you want to see how it all ends you could try 2 Kings.

Reflection on experience

Why does this piece of dialogue, which might be quite commonplace in a library in other circumstances, seem odd when we're talking about the Bible? Is it because we think we should start at the beginning and work through to the end; or because we think it has just one author, or perhaps some other reason? Come back to this question at the end of this session and see how appropriate the dialogue really seems in the light of what the chapter says.

Many people read the Old Testament as if:

- It had all been carefully planned in advance;
- All the writers knew that they were contributing to something that would one day be regarded as Holy Writ;
- The writers knew they were writing for future generations, especially ours;
- The words in the collection were designed to be written and read rather than spoken and heard;
- The writers all recognized that one day there would be a New Testament; and
- It were written in sequence from 'the beginning' to the end of the book of Malachi.

In fact, none of these assumptions is justified, and they all prevent us from accessing the material more easily. The Old Testament material spans around 700 years. Imagine if just now we were putting the finishing touches to a work that was begun in 1300 CE – and that's before the first recorded literary work in English! There is no way that such a work could be planned in advance, by the first writers. In fact the collection grew in a very haphazard way and according to principles that are not always clear to us. Probably none of the writers consciously believed that they were writing for future generations or that they were writing sacred documents in the sense that we now regard the Bible. They were writers in and for their own times. They certainly believed that what they were writing was significant and serious. They certainly wrote with the needs of their own faith community in view. They certainly regarded their work as being theological, in that it was about God and the ways that his activity could be discerned and understood in their times and societies. People nowadays write such books but would be amazed to find that in the year 4000 CE they were revered in a special collection.

It should be no surprise also, given the haphazard nature of the development of the Old Testament, that it does not appear in our Bibles in the sequence in which it was written. Some of the prophetic books (take Jeremiah for instance) were being written at much the same time, in the same cultural milieu and in awareness of the same issues as some of the books that look more like history (1 Kings for example); or that seem to belong to a much earlier period (like Deuteronomy). The very first chapter of the Bible is among the latest of its writings! The situation becomes even more complicated when we consider that some writings are composite, including work from different periods, incorporated over a substantial length of time.

So far we have spoken about 'authors' and 'works' as if we were talking about modern authors. That assumption is also false. Some of the works in the Old Testament 'took shape' over a very long period of time, and included a lot of material that had originally been handed on from generation to generation in spoken or oral form. Of the ones that perhaps were not, we know little or nothing about the lives of the individuals who were responsible for their final form. (We sometimes use the term 'final redactor' to describe this person.) Most of the works included in the collection were in fact not the work of isolated individuals at all, but rather of a group of people who had a particular 'take' on the religious quest. Among them are groups who had a particular interest in telling the story of Israel in a particular way to give sense and meaning to their present situation. Other groups were determined to preserve some of the (spoken) words of great orators, or prophets. Yet others were scholars or wise men writing, perhaps, as a kind of school offering a commentary on the observed world in the light of their religious faith. Perhaps the most serious misconception is that they wrote in the belief that there would one day be a New Testament. And that is not just because they did not even realize that there would be an Old Testament. The Hebrew scriptures are not simply the preserve of Christians. They form part of the sacred scriptures of the Jewish religion as well; and they inform the religion of Islam.

Perhaps one final false assumption might be that scholars have ready access to the answers to all the questions we might want to ask about the authors. In fact we actually know very little for certain. I remember in a New Testament class I was teaching where I was dealing with the fraught question of how we can know that the text of the Bible we have is correct and has not been corrupted in transmission, being asked, 'Why don't we just refer to the originals?' and by the way, 'Where are they kept?' The answer is that we have no originals. We only have copies that were made hundreds of years after the originals were produced. Our access to their original provenance and form is by a mixture of painstaking scholarship and inspired guesswork. One of the ways in which this study is conducted is called source criticism.

Historical critical methods

There are three main kinds of work involved in examining texts using the critical tools of historians. The assumption is that texts reach us in a final form that has undergone a number of changes, additions and corrections. The task is to unravel all that and set out the bits that have made up this composite whole, and to say something about the process that led to the final form of the text, perhaps even suggesting reasons why changes were made.

Source criticism is in a sense the final goal. This sets out to discover the main sources of a composite work. Source criticism was being developed particularly during the late nineteenth and early twentieth centuries.

Form criticism is interested in small pieces of text (sometimes called pericopae), which have something in common. By isolating these portions and classifying them scholars hope to throw light on their original context, as well as the process by which and the milieu in which they were brought together. This was common throughout the twentieth century.

Redaction criticism examines the circumstances in which the final edition, the one that we have, came into being. It is interested in the reasons why the units of material available to the editor or redactor were used in exactly the way they have been. This kind of criticism is nearest to literary critical method, and was developed from the mid-twentieth century onwards.

If we were looking at the first three Gospels in the New Testament:

- Source critics would be interested in which Gospel was used as a source for the other two.
- Form criticism would be looking at similar common material such as parables or miracle stories and asking about where they came from and how they were communicated.
- Redaction criticism would be asking why the author of, say, Luke used the particular material he did, and why he combined it in the way he did. They would wonder about the circumstances in his community which might call for this Gospel, and how they differed from those of the other Gospel writers.

At some point we may then ask, 'What does it mean, in the light of all this, to describe the Bible as the inspired word of God?' Surely such a description implies authorship, structure and purpose. Well, whatever we mean, we do not mean that these works were somehow dictated by God and simply written down. There are religious works that answer to such an understanding of inspiration, but the works in the Bible are not among them.

Reflection on experience

Think about how we use the word 'inspired'. Think of any situation in which you have used that description of written work. What did you mean? It may be you thought

- It had such universal significance that the meaning transcended the original author's own purpose;
- It had a power to change you that you were reluctant to ascribe to human ingenuity;
- It had a 'rightness' in the situation, and appeared to so fully understand the human condition that it appeared to transcend mere human imagination;
- God is 'behind it all' in some way that is difficult to define.

Is any of these an appropriate way of thinking about the Bible as inspired? Does your reflection have a bearing on your views about the authorship of the Bible?

Source criticism, as its name implies, is an attempt to unravel the writings of (in this case) the Old Testament, so as to try to determine

- How many authors there were,
- When they wrote,
- How their work might have become combined over a period to form larger composite pieces, and so perhaps,
- To offer ideas about why they wrote.

This was one of the earliest critical methods to be applied to the scriptures. It belongs to the historically based family of critical methods and was pursued, particularly by German scholars (of whom one of the most prominent was Julius Wellhausen, 1844–1918), during the eighteenth and nineteenth centuries. It appeared to shed lots of new light on how the Bible had been written – and especially those parts of it that seemed to come from several sources combined, such as the first three New Testament Gospels. The two immediate questions which source criticism raises are: (1) How do you begin to suspect that a document is composite? and (2) If you have identified a composite document, how do you begin to separate it into different strands?

Reflection on experience

Think about the first of these questions. What are the clues to a composite document? Think of a document you know to be the work of several hands. What are the give-aways? They might include:

- Very obvious differences of style
- Differences of emphasis
- Subtle inconsistencies and even contradictions
- Clumsy attempts at editing and harmonization.

Can you think of examples, or add your own criteria?

In the Old Testament the most obvious candidate for this kind of critical treatment was the Pentateuch – the first five books of the Bible – which, with the name Torah or Law, form the first distinctive part of the Hebrew Bible. It includes all the signs noted above and some others as well. One of the most obvious is the repetition of what might be considered the same material.

Reflection on text

Read Genesis1.1—2.3, then Genesis 2.4–25. These are both stories about creation, appearing to cover the same ground, but are entirely different and in some respects mutually contradictory. See how many differences you can find between them. Look at the style in which they are written; the order of events; the relative importance in the accounts of different bits of creation. In particular look at the status of humankind in each account. Does this crucial element differ and if so in what ways? What do you think each account is saying about the place of human beings in the overall scheme of things?

Alongside such blatant repetition and disagreement there are many examples of minor repetition. There are three accounts of a man pretending that his wife is actually his sister for example (Genesis 12.10–20, 20.1–18; 26.1–11). There are more important contradictions in the different accounts of how separate nations emerged (Genesis 10.31f. and Genesis 11.1–9) with consequential contradictions in the interpretation of the realities these accounts describe. Is it a good thing that there are separate nations and languages: a part of God's purpose, a natural consequence of his desire expressed in Genesis 1.28 to 'fill the earth' (as Genesis 10 would have us believe)? Or is it a bad thing: yet one more example of human sinfulness and rebellion leading to a compromise in the original plan of creation (as Genesis 11 wants us to think)? There do seem to be very different agendas at work here.

Exegesis

Exegesis is a way of thoroughly analysing the text so as to 'read out' from it an interpretation which is based on what that text originally meant to those who first produced, transmitted, valued or heard it. A typical modern exegetical handbook such as Douglas Stewart, *Exegesis: A Handbook for Students and Pastors* (2001) will help the reader formulate a process for achieving this based on an examination of several areas. For example:

- The proper translation of the text, taking account of the fact that nuances from the original Hebrew language may be lost in translation;
- The historical context of both writer and readers;
- The literary form chosen, and the literary context of the text in question, usually related, again, to the kind of life context (the German term often used to describe this is *Sitz im Leben*) which might have prompted it. For example, if the text is part of a religious ceremony, what kind of ceremony was it, and under what circumstances was it used?

The exegete usually wants to make connections between this work and the contemporary application of the text by asking questions about, for example,

- The theology of the text;
- The issues with which it deals;
- What critics have discerned from the text through the ages;
- The relation of the specific text to the Bible as a whole.

It is normally assumed that the end-product of this exegesis is some act of communicating to a contemporary audience through teaching or a sermon.

An alternative way of discerning the meaning of a text is eisegesis, which involves a 'reading into' the text from contemporary experience. This method is more compatible with literary forms of criticism.

But, having decided that a document is composite, how do you separate the strands? Again, it may be useful to reflect on how we might embark on that project with a modern document. We might identify continuous coherent sections in the work and see what they have in common. We might look for characteristic words or phrases or other idiosyncrasies of style. We might look for the emergence of a point of view that ties some sections together; or for sections which seem to display special interest in specific areas. Each of these criteria would be checked against the others. It was detective work of this kind, on the style and vocabulary of the Pentateuch, the first five books of the Old Testament, that led to the emergence of a theory which, though greatly changed from its original formulation, is, in important respects, still current today.

This theory is often referred to as the Documentary Hypothesis because it assumed that there were original documents on which the Pentateuch drew, and it identified four of them. It also attempted to relate them to different periods in the history of Israel, and to different stages of development in the religion of Israel. Some of the convictions that drove the work are now contested. For example:

- The idea of a continuous development of the religion of Israel towards fulfilment in Christ is now seen as misjudged.
- It is recognized that talk of 'documents' is misplaced in a situation in which a variety of means of transmitting tradition, including oral ones, were employed.
- There is less confidence now that it is possible to identify specific stages in the development of the tradition. The original four-document hypothesis was challenged as being too simple a description of that process, and scholars vied with each other to produce ever more involved accounts of how the sources came into being and evolved. Thus, the four-document thesis led to work which so fragmented the Pentateuch that it became of interest only to people who collect stamps.

However, some basic principles from the original idea do survive, and they include a general fourfold division, related to historic periods, which are reckoned to inform us as to how the theology of the Old Testament lived and grew.

The first of the four sources is called J because this source uses the word 'Yahweh' (which in German transliteration begins with J) as God's name. This, the oldest source, probably derives from the tenth century BCE. Depending on your point of reference you might think of this as the early Iron Age (if you were an archaeologist), or the early monarchical period, that is, the period when Israel began to be ruled by kings (if you were an historian). Among the special features of this source is the intimacy between God and humankind, and the interest in the questions about the limits of human power. In the Garden of Eden, God speaks to Adam 'man to man' (Genesis 2.16f.) and walks about in the cool of the day, expecting a close encounter (3.8ff.). When the people of Babel build a tower, God comes down to look at it (Genesis 11.5). This source also uses extended narrative and storytelling as the chosen means of conveying the message, with considerable artistry (see for example Genesis 38).

The second source is called E for similar reasons. This source uses the word 'Elohim' as the name of God. Slightly later than J, perhaps ninth century BCE, this source displays a greater distance between humanity and God. God no longer speaks intimately with humans but rather appears to them in dreams (Genesis 20.3; 28.12; 40.5ff.) or through angels or intermediaries (Genesis 32.1). This too is to some extent a storytelling source in some ways parallel to that of J. Unlike J, which derives from the south of the country, E comes from the north, though that may have little significance for us. But this source does have an interest in moral questions in terms of duty and individual responsibility and is responsible, for example, for the description of the lawgiving at Sinai (Exodus 20.1–17). The theory suggests that a little later, but before the seventh century BCE, these two sources were combined to form JE. Some of the most entertaining stories from the book of Genesis in particular are a combination of these two sources.

A third source came into being at the end of the seventh and beginning of the sixth centuries BCE. In biblical history this is the period when Israel ceases to be ruled by its own monarchs and begins to be conquered, occupied or worse by a succession of foreign powers. This source is called D since its main work is the production of the book of Deuteronomy. This source has a particular interest in the special relationship between God and Israel, and what each side needs to do and understand in order to make the relationship prosper. It has a preaching style and uses the second person frequently. The final source, which contains less narrative (i.e. storytelling) material, and more stylized writing in other genres, is called P. This stands for writings that derived from a Priestly environment, and which was probably complete before the end of the fifth century BCE. Most of the material in the books of Leviticus and Numbers derive from this source. The style is dry and the source includes lots of lists, genealogies and detailed instructions about how to observe liturgical ceremonies. That being said, don't give up on P. In many ways it is the most interesting of the sources, theologically, and contains fascinating insights into the human situation, as we shall see. Source criticism did not stop at the Pentateuch. The books which run in most Bibles from Joshua through to 2 Kings are considered to come from the same stable as the book of Deuteronomy and for that reason are sometimes called the Deuteronomistic Histories. Similarly the two books of Chronicles, together with Ezra and Nehemiah, are thought to be associated with the P school. This raises fascinating questions about what these several sources believed so passionately, and yet so differently, about God and his relationship with the world that they were inspired to write about them.

JEDP

Photocopy the text of Genesis 35 and highlight the text in different ways to identify the three sources J, E and P.

1–4, (E), 5 (P), 6–8 (E), 9–13 (P), 14 (J) 15(P) 16–22a (J), 22b–29 (P)

Source criticism is not always an exact science but this division into the three sources J, E and P, however approximate, illustrates (a) the complexity of the unravelling process, and (b) something of the distinctiveness of the sources. An example of the repetition characteristic of composite documents is to be found in v. 15. When you read this verse you think, 'Didn't we know this already? Wasn't this assumed at the beginning of the chapter?' Verses 16–22 form a continuous short story dealing with a bit of history that happened in the (southern) Bethlehem area. This is J's main contribution. E is more concerned for things that happened in the north (around Shechem). P characteristically uses the name 'Israel' instead of Jacob and introduces that in this passage. When God speaks to Jacob/Israel it is in a liturgical poetic form. The genealogy at the end of the passage is also typical of the P source.

The work of source critics had two main effects. First, it encouraged people to see that when new critical methods were applied to the Bible, they could yield results that enabled a better-informed reading, which in turn allowed people to make more sense of what they read. Second, it showed that interesting insights could be gained by relating writers, authors or sources, to historic events and backgrounds. Although the kind of correspondence between text and history which people like Wellhausen argued for is no longer fashionable, it is still thought important to be able to relate the two in some way, in order to answer the question with which we began this chapter: Why did the writers write? If their words were not just dictated by God in some kind of history-free zone, then they must have been prompted by their experiences and context. Now, you might think that it would be a relatively simple matter to take each of these sources J, E, D and P, and to ask what was happening in the history of Israel at the time they were produced, which could have spurred them to write. But as we shall see later, that's more complicated than it appears. Nevertheless, it is possible to tell the story of Israel in a way that makes some sense both of what we know of its history, and of what we know of its texts, that does give us a real handle on the material, and begins to give us insight into why people still read this stuff with so much enthusiasm.

CHAPTER 3 SUMMARY

What is this chapter about?

Building on the work of the first two chapters, this chapter is an introduction to the idea of a canon of scripture. As well as listing the books of the Old Testament, the chapter looks at the various ways they have been organized, and the implications of the differences. Finally the chapter looks at alternative modern ways of getting a handle on the material as a whole.

What books are referred to?

The only new work referred to in the text is Stephen Dempster, *Dominion and Dynasty* (Leicester: IVP, 2001).

What other books would be helpful?

The Brueggemann introduction (2003) is particularly aware of the issues raised in this chapter. The works of B. S. Childs also have a special interest in the concept of canon, including: *Biblical Theology in Crisis* (1970); Commentary on Exodus (1974); *Introduction to the Old Testament as Scripture* (1979); *Old Testament Theology in a Canonical Context* (1985) and *Biblical Theology of the Old and New Testaments* (1992). Of these the most accessible is the commentary on Exodus. A simple introduction is provided by John Barton, *Making the Christian Bible* (London: Darton, Longman & Todd, 1997).

How is the chapter organized?

The main topics for this chapter are as follows: the relationship between organization and meaning; the main sections and sub-sections of the Hebrew Bible; the arrangement of books in Christian Bibles today; using the Exodus as an organizing principle in reading; using the Exile as an organizing principle in reading; the implications of both these approaches.

What should I be able to do by the end of this chapter?

Recount the contents of the Old Testament, and the various arrangements of them.

Recognize the implications of different reading strategies.

Understand that as a matter of presentation, the way books are organized affects their meaning.

3

Are the Books in the Right Order?

By modern standards, the Old Testament is a public relations presentation disaster. Given the material it includes, no modern PR executive would dream of presenting it in this form. Nowadays, anything so complicated would have a lengthy introduction; a guide as to how to read it, and a list of FAQs and reader helps just to make sure we didn't get lost on the way. But beyond those most basic things the material would be grouped together differently. Key points and central ideas would be identified. Interesting bits would be highlighted. Different kinds of material would be given different priority, and in all likelihood, a great deal of it would actually be relegated to a series of appendices. The problem with such an approach is, that what one person thinks is a key idea or an interesting bit, might be disputed by another. To rearrange the material is to interpret it. And yet the arrangement of some, at least, of the material is according to conscious decision. We have already seen for example how the P, or Priestly, writers took existing work and edited and reworked it. We see in their work an attempt to present a point of view, a theology, an argument. It is important to realize then that asking questions about the order of the books is a way of asking about what the final redactors, editors or compilers wanted readers to believe.

Reflection on experience

One example of how choosing parts of the Old Testament, in an attempt to précis it, results in an individual interpretation, is designing a service of nine lessons and carols. Many people's understanding of what the Old Testament is about is informed by such a presentation. A more involved example might be the verses chosen by G. F. Handel for his *Messiah* oratorio. Both of these examples demonstrate a particular interpretation of how the Bible should be read in order for it to yield its main message. If you are familiar with these or other similar examples reflect for a moment on what they are saying the Bible is about. It might be useful to write this down and refer back to it at a later stage.

Actually, to call this collection 'The Old Testament', is itself an interpretation and organization of the material. Such a title assumes that there is to be a sequel, a New Testament, somehow related to this work, which is of course what Christians believe. Followers of Judaism have a different 'take' on all this. For them, what we are talking about is the Hebrew scriptures. The Hebrew scriptures are in fact divided into three groups. The first group is called 'Torah', which means 'law' or 'teaching'. This consists of the first five books of the Bible or the Pentateuch. The second group is called 'Nebiim' or prophets. This group is in turn subdivided into Former Prophets and Latter Prophets. This subdivision means little to us, since the books in the former category look more like history than prophecy, though they do contain accounts of how prophecy developed. The larger group contains the work of the better-known individual prophets such as Isaiah and Jeremiah. The final group is called the 'Ketubim' or Writings. From the first letters of these three Hebrew words followers of Judaism make the word 'TaNaK' which is the Jewish name for what Christians refer to as the Old Testament.

The Hebrew canon

The Torah
Genesis
Exodus
Leviticus
Numbers
Deuteronomy

The Prophets
The Former Prophets
  Joshua
  Judges
  Samuel
  Kings
The Latter Prophets
  Isaiah
  Jeremiah
  Ezekiel
  The Twelve Prophets

The Writings
Psalms
Proverbs
Job
Song of Songs
Ruth
Lamentations
Ecclesiastes
Esther
Daniel
Ezra
Nehemiah
Chronicles

This threefold division reflects the order in which the books reached their final form. We know that the Torah was complete by the fourth century BCE because it is used by both Samaritans and Jews, who split at that time. The Prophets section was complete by around 180 BCE, since Ecclesiasticus or Sirach, which was completed around that time, contains a continuous narrative section (46.1 to 49.10) which makes reference to the entire contents of the Former and Latter Prophets. Law and Prophets were the two sections of Hebrew scripture that were regarded as holy writ at the time of Jesus. Hence he refers to 'The Law and the Prophets' in appeal to scripture. (See for example Matthew 5.17; 7.12; 11.13; 22.40; Luke 16.16; 24.27.) The Writings were added to this twofold collection about sixty years after Jesus was crucified, though they contained works that were complete before his birth. It is likely that the final agreement as to which writings to include was reached by rabbis at the Synod of Jamnia in the last decade of the first century CE.

As we have already seen, the **Pentateuch**, the Torah section of the Hebrew Bible, is a composite work. It contains teaching about the foundations of Israel (see Chapter 8), which it conveys, both through telling stories about how and why Israel was formed, and by setting out some of the codes and principles that would determine its character and polity. Among the best known of the codes are:

- The **Decalogue** (Exodus 20.1–17) sometimes called the Ten Commandments, or, as in the original Hebrew, the Ten Words. A recent suggestion has also been made that they be called the Ten Commitments, on which see Chapter 7.
- The **Book of the Covenant** (Exodus 21—23), which sets out in more detail some of the implications and consequences of the Decalogue in everyday life.
- The **Ritual Decalogue** (Exodus 34), which relates the Decalogue to religious observance.
- The **Holiness Code** (Leviticus 17—26). This code, some source critics describe as H because it appears to form a definite block of material, consistent with but distinct from the P material which makes up most of the book. Its emphasis is that the people of God must reflect the holiness of God if they are to live happily in a land that has been polluted by sin.
- The **Deuteronomic Code** (Deuteronomy 5—26). This series of sermon-like exhortations sets out a kind of constitution for Israel based on the particular relationship the authors see between God and his people, the Covenant. The laws are placed in a theological framework conveyed by story and saga which seek to describe who God is, in relation to the world, humankind and human society.

Reflection on text

Read Exodus 20.1–17 and then read Exodus 34.1–5, 10–28. The conclusion of the source critics is that the first passage is essentially from the E source. The second is the earlier J source. The final editors or redactors preferred to give E top billing. Why do you think they did that, and has anything been lost by concentrating on the very stark presentation of the Decalogue in Exodus 20?

The **Prophets** section of the Hebrew Bible is also a bit of a surprise. The **Former Prophets** contains largely narrative. The books of Samuel and Kings do give insight into how prophecy developed. In the early days, prophecy was the work of anonymous groups of officials, and we do hear something about that, but almost by accident as these books appear to have a different agenda altogether, telling the tales of a succession of kings. The **Latter Prophets** speak of later times when individuals, sometimes isolated and reviled, uttered memorable oracles. These books contain some narrative but much more oracle – the recorded sayings of particular prophets in particular situations, often in a kind of poetic form. The story of how prophecy developed is a fascinating one and we shall deal with it in Chapter 9. The succession of books from Joshua through to 2 Kings is a connected narrative, which has a strong ideological resemblance to the book of Deuteronomy. It is sometimes called the Deuteronomistic History or D History. We shall look at this view in more detail in Chapter 7. Within that history, 2 Samuel 9— 1 Kings 2 is a discrete section dealing with court intrigues which lead to David's downfall and the beginning of Solomon's reign. This is variously known as the Court narrative or the Succession narrative. Its contents would compete with any current soap on British television. What sometimes surprises people is that in the Bible, prophets are not people with tea leaves and a crystal ball, setting out a series of predictions in the style of *Old Moore's Almanac*, newspaper horoscopes, or in a personal 'You're about to go on a journey and meet a tall dark handsome stranger' kind of way.

The **Writings** are much more diverse in character. They include five short scrolls or 'Megilloth', each of which is still read aloud on specific Jewish festivals. They are Song of Songs (eighth day of Passover), Ruth (Pentecost), Lamentations (on the anniversary of the destruction of Jerusalem, on the Ninth Ab), Ecclesiastes (at the feast of Tabernacles) and Esther (at the feast of Purim). These five short books follow the book of Job in the Hebrew Bible. This book, along with Proverbs forms the core of Wisdom writing in the Old Testament (on which see Chapters 13, 15 and 18). Chronicles, Ezra and Nehemiah are an alternative account of the events narrated in the Deuteronomistic history, from a different standpoint and at a later time. The book of Daniel belongs to a special category called apocalyptic (see Chapter 14), and Psalms contains 150 poetic liturgical pieces (for more on which see Chapter 16).

Some scholars believe that the original purpose of the Old Testament is only evident through this threefold division (so for example recently Stephen Dempster, *Dominion and Dynasty* (2001). But when the Hebrew Bible was later translated into Greek, a different fourfold order was adopted which blurred the original three divisions. The aim appears to have been to group similar kinds of material, and to disperse the Writings throughout the rest of the books. So we have an arrangement, followed in English Bibles, which appears to group: the Pentateuch, the Historical writings, the Prophetic books and the Wisdom writings. This is a very loose categorization which does not automatically make reading any easier. To do that we need some

Law Books	Poetry and Wisdom Books
Genesis	Job
Exodus	Psalms
Leviticus	Proverbs
Numbers	Ecclesiastes
Deuteronomy	Song of Solomon
History Books	**Books of Prophecies**
Joshua	Isaiah
Judges	Jeremiah
Ruth	Lamentations
1 Samuel	Ezekiel
2 Samuel	Daniel
1 Kings	Hosea
2 Kings	Joel
1 Chronicles	Amos
2 Chronicles	Obadiah
Ezra	Jonah
Nehemiah	Micah
Esther	Nahum
	Habakkuk
	Zephaniah
	Haggai
	Zechariah
	Malachi

kind of underlying theme or narrative to which the different books can be related. We need a *handle*, a *guiding principle*.

A strong contender for the role of Old Testament handle is provided by the biblical account of the **Exodus**, and all that that involves. This story (see Chapter 6) describes the liberation of the people of Israel from slavery in Egypt, and their journeying through the desert to a new land of their own. This is a story about freedom and about salvation – saving a people from oppression and death. It is also a story about how God kept his promises made to the ancestors or patriarchs of Israel that they would have a special relationship with God; that they would have lots of descendants and that they would have a land of their own. This series of promises was God's side of an agreement entered into with the people of Israel called the Covenant. The terms of this agreement as far as the people were concerned were also set out during the Exodus, at Mount Sinai, as described at, for example Exodus 20—24. Very important themes for the religion of Judaism and Christianity are caught up in this account. They include: law, land, promise and fulfilment, sacrifice, journey, salvation, obedience and rebellion, trust and faith – to mention but a few. They also suggest to us important things about the way the people of Israel understood God, as a God who wants to make relationships, and wants those relationships to be based on love. God's own love and faithfulness lead to an understanding of his grace and capacity to give. On any account these are weighty themes and we shall encounter them many times. But do they give us the handle we are looking for to organize our reading of the Old Testament?

If we take the Exodus as our starting-point, then the books of the Pentateuch are core documents setting out the promises God made and the way in which they came to the brink of fulfilment. They also set out the terms of the Covenant at Mount Sinai. They should be read first, to understand what are the core traditions of Israel. In subsequent generations we shall then read about how those traditions are interpreted afresh. More importantly perhaps, we shall also see something of the failure of the people of Israel to live up to the agreement. The history books tell us about how things progressed till the time of the Exile, which came about as a result of failure to live as a Covenant people should. The Prophetic books from before the Exile warn the people about their increasing distance from what God wants of them. The prophetic books written at the time of the Exile and afterwards show once again that God is forgiving and generous. Once again he is willing to rescue his people from their predicament as slaves in a foreign land and establish them in his promised land. This cycle of rebellion and return, of sin and forgiveness, then becomes a pattern, a model, which allows us to understand the basic thrust of salvation in Christianity. People who rebel and contravene the will of God are nevertheless forgiven. God's love, evidenced in a number of ways – some of them very painful and involving suffering – saves people not just from oppression as slaves but from the slavery of sin. The Writings section then includes worship resources to accompany this developing understanding of God's way with his people, and wisdom writings which allow a more philosophical perspective on the whole story.

This way of understanding the story of the Old Testament has a number of advantages:

- It allows us to read the Old Testament more or less in the order in which it is set out in our Bibles.
- It gives us opportunity to explore the development of a single theme which is undoubtedly extremely important.
- It gives us one way of relating the story of the Old Testament to our own lives and experience.
- It seems to accord with the way in which the people of Israel themselves came to know more about God as a saving God.

However, it is not the only possible handle, and in recent years a kind of alternative has been suggested, which is based on our increasing understanding of when the books reached their final form. This alternative model, this alternative way of reading and understanding the Old Testament, is based not on the Exodus, but on the Exile.

Reflection on text

Read 2 Kings 25.1–26. This is an account of the last days of Judah, and the beginning of the Exile. Imagine yourself as an Israelite who wants to maintain your faith in the face of all that is happening. What is most shocking to you in this account, and how might you make sense of it?

The basic premise, if we read the Old Testament in this way, is that the Old Testament as we know it only came into being after the Exile, and in a sense owes its existence to that Exile experience. If we tell the story in this way we begin with that experience. In 597 and 587 respectively two traumatic events took place which are described in the book of Jeremiah, and so in a sense that is where this way of reading would begin. In those years the nation of Israel, which had already been seriously weakened when the northern part of the nation had been overrun by the Assyrians in 722, was now completely overcome by the nation of Babylon. All the movers and shakers of the nation were forcibly removed and marched to captivity and exile in Babylon. To all intents and purposes Israel ceased to exist as a nation. To people who had been brought up on the notion that they were chosen and precious to God, this was the ultimate religious disaster, prompting the question: How could God let this happen? At the time of the Exile a group of religious radicals set about answering this question. They were aware of ancient traditions (J and E), which set out the basis of the covenant agreement, but were unhappy with the way it had been interpreted and assimilated into the life of the nation. The prophet Jeremiah was one of this group. They set about writing a history of Israel, which demonstrated that the question 'How could God let this happen?' could be answered quite simply. It was the people's fault, or more specifically, it was the fault of the rulers and leaders of Israel. This history appears in our Bibles as the Deuteronomistic history (that is, the books from Joshua through to 2 Kings). This group, which also treasured the words of the prophets of the eighth century such as Amos and Micah, didn't stop there. They set out a kind of constitution for Israel which described what Israel would be like if it really took the Covenant seriously. This is our book of Deuteronomy.

At some point during the Exile (which lasted until about 539) things began to change. There seemed to be a new possibility that the people could return from exile, and this is what happened to some of them when the Babylonian empire was itself conquered by the Persians. The message then changed from reflection on blame and repentance, to hope for the future. We read about this in the book of Ezekiel, and in Isaiah 40—55. Eventually, some, though not all, the Israelites (now called Jews) did return and faced the daunting prospect of starting life afresh. A new history was called for, from this new perspective, which would answer the question, not 'How could God let this happen?' but rather, 'How can we survive and grow as the people of God in this new situation?' This new history is 1 and 2 Chronicles, Ezra and Nehemiah. Other prophets, such as Haggai, continued to offer commentary on the new task.

But the experience of exile had actually changed the religious outlook of the people. They had come to understand new things about God. Slowly the realization became current that God was not just the best of many gods; a God whose influence only extended to the borders of Israel. If he could so organize international affairs, and really be with his people in the foreign land of Babylon then their understanding of God had been incomplete. He was in fact, as they now came to realize, the only God. This brought new challenges. If God were the only God then he was God of all creation. If he were the only God then he had organized and designed not only creation but also human history. If he were the only God then he was God of all peoples. Later books of the Old Testament then represent a grappling with these new understandings. If God is the God of all creation then it must be possible to see something of the creator in all aspects of his creation – so we have books like Proverbs, which explore observable aspects of that creation. If God is the God who designed history then a new kind of theological work was called for which unpacked the whole question of the historical destiny of the world. Daniel is an example of such a work. If God is the God of all peoples then he has an interest in people other than the Jews – the message of the book of Jonah – and urges Israel to a more inclusive and generous view of other nations – the message of the book of Ruth.

But it isn't all adventurous and positive. If God is the God of creation and history, why did he design things this way? And in particular why is there sorrow in the world? Why is there evil and suffering in the world? How can one believe in and worship God in a world that seems so at odds with his revealed character? This is part of the thinking behind the book of Job. Alongside all this are the priestly writers, aware of all these new experiences, possibilities and questions, who then edit and complete the Pentateuch to take account of it all. This too represents a way of reading the Old Testament that has advantages. For example:

- It takes seriously the circumstances in which the final editions of the books were produced.
- It enables a more convincing rationale of the relationship of some of the writings, particularly the wisdom literature, to the rest of the Old Testament.
- It offers a starting-point for interpretation, which is accessible to the modern experiences of rootlessness, loneliness, god-forsakenness, alienation, and post-traumatic anxiety that many people today would want to call experiences of a kind of exile.
- It is not mutually exclusive with a way of reading that considers the theme of Exodus centrally important.

Some people have wanted to combine these two approaches. The Exile approach and story tells us *why* the books reached their final form in the way they did. The Exodus approach and story tells us *what story* those people wanted us to hear. However, this is not good enough for those who want to see in the Old Testament a straightforward unfolding of history, with a narrative based on report of what really happened. They would still think of the Exile as being near the end of the story rather than at its beginning, and would be unhappy to think that the account of the Exodus and conquest of Canaan, followed by the settlement into the promised land, was manipulated and presented in a form which owed something to events hundreds of years after the Exodus. Clearly then, questions about history and the Old Testament are central and important.

CHAPTER 4 SUMMARY

What is this chapter about?

This chapter continues with the question 'How ought we to read the Bible?' by looking at the relationship between the biblical accounts and actual history, with all the critical implications of such study. In particular it charts what is a current and heated debate about the issues around what we can know about history, what we need to know, and whether and to what extent historical fact is reflected in the writings of the Old Testament.

What books are referred to?

The following new books are referred to:

H. J. Richards, *The First Christmas: What Really Happened?* (London: Fontana, 1973) and *The First Easter: What Really Happened?* (London: Fontana, 1976). P. R. Davies, *In Search of 'Ancient Israel'* (Sheffield: JSOT Press, 1992); K. Whitelam, *The Invention of Ancient Israel* (London: Routledge, 1996); William G. Dever, *What Did the Biblical Writers Know and When Did They Know It?* (Grand Rapids, Mich.: Eerdmans, 2001) and *Who Were the Early Israelites and Where Did They Come From?* (Grand Rapids, Mich.: Eerdmans, 2003); I. Finkelstein, *The Archaeology of the Israelite Settlement* (Jerusalem: Israel Exploration Society, 1988); N. Gottwald, *The Tribes of Yahweh* (London: SCM Press, 1979); W. Albright, 'The Israelite conquest in the light of archaeology', in *Bulletin of the American Schools of Oriental Research* 74 (1939), pp. 11–22; A. Alt, 'The settlement of the Israelites in Palestine', trans. R. Wilson, in *Essays on Old Testament History and Religion* (Garden City, NY: Doubleday 1968); M. Noth, *The History of Israel*, 2nd edn (London: Blackwell, 1960); Leo G. Perdue (ed.), *The Blackwell Companion to the Hebrew Bible* (Oxford: Blackwell, 2001), for: C. E. Carter, 'Social scientific approaches', pp. 36–53, and Carol Meyers, 'Early Israel and the rise of the Israelite monarchy' pp. 61–86.

What other books would be helpful?

The list above is pretty exhaustive and points to a lively current debate. Commentary is offered by John J. McDermott, *What Are They Saying about the Formation of Israel?* (New York: Paulist Press, 1998), which gives further bibliography. On biblical archaeology, a useful introduction is Volkmar Fritz, *An Introduction to Biblical Archaeology* (Sheffield: JSOT Press, 1994). A good introduction to the implications of the debate for reading the historical books of the Old Testament is Mary Mills, *Historical Israel: Biblical Israel* (London: Cassell, 1999).

How is the chapter organized?

The chapter begins with an examination of the issues around the current debate about the importance of history. This is followed by a section on the contribution of archaeology and one on the contribution of sociology. There is discussion about the conquest of Israel as a test case. The chapter concludes with a summary of the main points.

What should I be able to do by the end of this chapter?

Understand the implications of relating the biblical narrative to historical events.

Distinguish between competing views in the current debate on these issues and participate intelligently.

4

What Really Happened: How Do We Know, and Does It Really Matter?

In the 1970s there appeared a series of books on the interpretation of the New Testament Gospels, each of which had the subtitle: What Really Happened? They included for example H. J. Richards's *The First Christmas: What Really Happened?* (1973) and *The First Easter: What Really Happened?* (1976). The books accepted that the question of what really happened is one which modern western readers think important, but argued that actually it is an inappropriate question to ask of the Gospel texts. They were not meant to be read as accounts of what happened. Rather, it was argued, they were complex and sophisticated theological documents presenting arguments about the significance of Jesus in an idiom and culture which is now largely lost to us. That being so, the real task should be to try and access that idiom and culture afresh, in order to read the Gospels more intelligently. H. J. Richards was only describing what was generally accepted in the academic theological community, yet he knew that what he wrote might come as a shock to those whose faith was based on believing that certain things happened in exactly the way described. A similar process has been under way for some time with regard to the Old Testament, but there appears an even greater reticence about sharing the insights gained because there seems to be so much at stake in the way Christian and Jewish communities, especially, view the Old Testament as a record of history.

Reflection on experience

How important is it for you to know that certain things in the Bible really happened? Are there different categories of 'event' that assume different levels of importance? Consider the following list taken from the narrative sections of the Old Testament. Are any of them crucial, at this stage? Look at the list again having considered the arguments of this chapter.

- God created Adam and Eve in the Garden of Eden
- God sent a series of plagues on the people of Egypt
- God rescued the Israelites from slavery and led them to a land of their own
- God helped the people drive out the population of the land of Canaan so that it could be their land instead.

For the most part, historical considerations have a small role in the current interpretation of the *New* Testament. When you open a book on how to read the New Testament you will rarely be treated to a survey of the historical events against which the drama of Jesus' life and death were played out. There appears little need to know which kings ruled, or the exact extent of their kingdoms. We remain unaware of which Roman emperors made decisions in relation to Palestine and how the Roman system was organized. Latterly there has been a development of interest in the sociological background of the New Testament – what it felt like to live in one of the cities addressed by Paul, or what was the social background of the disciples, or what was the place of women in society at the time, and so on – but the political history remains largely untold. All this is very different from the approach of those who have introduced the *Old* Testament to us. Almost without exception, until recently, they have begun with an account of the history of Israel, on the basis that none of the rest of the writings makes sense without knowing that. Now, that is changing.

At the extreme edge of this change in scholarship is a group of writers who believe not only that it is useful to study the Old Testament with the critical tools appropriate to the study of literature but, rather, that it is important to accept that the Old Testament is in fact *literature*, and that to subject it to critical methods as if it were history is to produce gross distortions. Philip Davies' *In Search of Ancient Israel* (1992) is widely regarded as the first systematic publication of this view. He in fact distinguishes three 'Israels'. One of them is historical Israel. This is the actual history of actual people in actual places, in Davies' view largely inaccessible through the biblical text. Biblical Israel, on the other hand, is a kind of historical novel set against the background of these people and events, rather in the manner of one of Shakespeare's Roman or history plays or (as Davies himself says) *A Tale of Two Cities*. As you might expect in such a work, there are connections between actual history and this literary fiction (or literary construct as he calls it) but that does not give biblical Israel historical credibility as such. In fact, as his title suggests, Davies' main interest is in 'Ancient Israel', the third on his list. This is, if you like, the Israel which biblical scholars and faith communities alike talk about, write about and have in mind in their devotions. In Davies' analysis it results from a huge mistake – the mistake of treating the literary creation of *biblical* Israel as if it were an exact representation of *historical* Israel.

Davies believes that most writing about the history of Israel is based on a kind of circular argument that assumes from the start what it claims to prove by rational means. He believes it better to abandon any attempt at historical reconstruction based on biblical record, and to regard the Old Testament as literature pure and simple. That leads him to questions about when and why it was written, and by whom. His conclusion is that it was written from the fifth century BCE onwards, after the deportation to Babylon and the return to Israel (though, of course, he has questions about the historicity of these 'events'), as part of a project to define national and religious identity; and that it was actually composed in a series of temple scribal 'Colleges'. He believes that the presumed 'ownership' of the texts by faith communities and theologians has silenced the kind of critique he is making, and that political considerations have had a part to play during the last hundred years or so as a new country called Israel has once again emerged in the region. The subtitle of a work from the same school, Keith Whitelam's *The Invention of Ancient Israel: The Silencing of Palestinian History* (1996), shows what is at stake here.

The discussions engendered by the work of this school have been heated and adversarial, but the lines of debate are not quite as clear-cut as you might expect. This is not a history-versus-literature debate, exactly, nor a debate about the verbatim recording of facts over against a fictional construct. There is a widespread acceptance in the scholarly community of the following.

1. The biblical account does move fairly rapidly, and without indication, from legend to alleged history. The early chapters of Genesis speak of people called Adam and Eve, but few believe they are, or are meant to be understood as, historical figures. Genesis chapter 6 describes how the 'sons of the Gods' took human wives for themselves. There is widespread scepticism about whether there was an actual person called Noah or even Abraham. Whatever it means to say that Moses spoke with God on a mountain, or that seas parted, or that rivers turned to blood, it is clear that we are not dealing with observable phenomena with which we can make any connection with our experience. Critics have been long aware that **myth** and **legend** play their part in the descriptions and have tried to understand how this kind of writing operates in primitive societies. One writer puts it thus: 'In legend and saga we have the historiography of peoples who have not yet reached the stage of mature history-writing and who therefore lack the capacity for synthesis and choice which is to be found among those who have arrived historically at a certain level of maturity' (Soggin 1976, pp. 49f.).

2. History writing is a complicated and sophisticated enterprise. History is rarely either naive or disinterested. People write history for a reason and present their readers with an argument. Histories of the same 'events' differ widely depending on the viewpoint of the author, precisely because they are intimately connected to the author's present. Indeed, people with the same basic sympathies and from the same community may write two completely different histories of the same period depending on how they want to make those connections, what the perceived needs of the authors' communities are – what questions they want answered – and the lessons they want to draw from them.

Reflection on text

Read 1 Samuel 8.10–21. Then read 1 Samuel 9.15f. and 10.1. These are two completely different responses to the question as to whether Israel should have a king. The first sets out all the disadvantages and suggests that God is against the idea. The second suggests that it's what God wants. The final editor has allowed these two accounts to stand side by side. What does that suggest to you about:

- The historical truth of what really happened?
- How the final editor of the book wants us to react?

The most obvious example from the Old Testament itself is the Deuteronomistic history on the one hand (the books from Joshua to 2 Kings), and the history of the Chronicler (1 and 2 Chronicles, together with Ezra and Nehemiah) on the other (see Chapters 7 and 17). These appear to give an account of the same events during the same period but are written at different times and from different standpoints, presenting different arguments to their readers and trying to answer different questions. They stand as *alternative* histories within the Old Testament.

3. Even if there is no dispute about the facts, they can be placed within completely different frameworks of meaning by different authors. To take a more modern example: in 1904 there occurred in a small village called Loughor in South Wales what has come to be known as the beginnings of a 'Revival'. Based on one small chapel there, and associated with the leadership of the Revd Evan Roberts, huge numbers of people quite unexpectedly turned to religion. There was a huge spin-off of religious interest, new religious phenomena, such as charismatic utterance, were observed and new chapels had to be built to cope. It is possible to describe this in terms of social conditions at the time. You might draw attention to a new sense of human fragility occasioned by the recent incidence of a cholera outbreak, a new impatience among the young to have a voice in public affairs, political consciousness associated with the rise of the Labour movement, and so on. Church historians tend to describe it in a different way. They make connections with great Revivals

of the past, such as the Methodist Revival and see it as a miracle. Indeed, there are religious bodies today who base their vision and strategy for the present (especially around the anniversary of these events) on that understanding. Their prayers are for a new Revival which they would then understand as being part of this great 'historical' tradition. As far as these people are concerned this is what 'really' happened. The sociological or political analysis are but symptoms of this great purpose. The whole genre of apocalyptic writing (see further Chapter 14) interprets relatively innocuous events as part of a great design for history, and claims that the significance of the events can only 'really' be seen in this way.

4. Historically based methods of criticism themselves accept a process within tradition, such that a degree of creative reinterpretation took place. This is one of the inevitable results of source and form criticism. The ultimate form of historically based methods, **redaction criticism,** concludes that a degree of creative work was done by the final editors of the texts, as they sought to provide a framework within their own arguments in which to place the traditions they had received.

However, none of this resolves the basic questions:

• about whether these texts are meant to be read as history or literature;
• about the relationship between the 'facts' – the historical Israel – and what we read in the Old Testament; and
• about whether the final edition of the texts, which is commonly believed to derive from a relatively late period, was based on traditions which date back to the times they describe or whether they were new inventions.

Meanwhile, two other academic disciplines have been bringing their insights to bear on questions relating to the Old Testament and history. One is archaeology and the other is sociology. They have been concerned in the first place with historical Israel (as Davies would describe it), and with the lives and cultures of the people of the Palestinian highlands during the Late Bronze Age and Early Iron Age. In general, the important conclusions that many, though not all, of these studies reach is, that the traditions embedded in the Old Testament text in its final form could well derive from much earlier periods than that at which the final form emerged. In other words, the final text could include much earlier traditions that do spring from the contexts they describe. They also conclude that, not only is it unnecessary to dismiss the historicity of Old Testament writings as compositions from scratch at a late period, but that to do so flies in the face of evidence which they claim archaeology and sociology provide. (William G. Dever would be one example of an archaeologist who has taken up cudgels in this fight.) This puts them very much at odds with the views of Davies et al., whom they characteristically describe as 'reductionists'. However, that is not to proclaim a victory for the view that history is, after all, naive and disinterested. In fact these disciplines have themselves reached conclusions about historical Israel which would be regarded as very challenging to traditional views. Among them is the commonly held view that the Exodus and Entry into the Promised Land did not take place in the way the Bible describes it; and indeed the view that the twelve tribes of Israel were not descendants of Jacob, and were not in fact ethnically related at all.

The ways in which the findings of archaeologists have been used by Old Testament scholars have changed enormously during the last hundred and fifty years or so. As critical methods came to be applied to the Bible, which seemed to undermine its contents as literal truth, archaeology was thought of by some as an ally to prove that what the Bible said had happened had really happened. When critics said that stories such as the great flood (Genesis 6—9) or the destruction of Sodom and Gomorrah (Genesis 19.1–29), or the destruction of Jericho (Joshua 6) were, to an extent, legendary creations, so-called biblical archaeologists set to work to prove them wrong. After all, they thought, it ought to be possible to find some archaeological evidence for destruction on the scale of the Genesis accounts. Indeed, I saw a TV programme recently, describing a modern attempt to locate Sodom and Gomorrah which went into considerable detail about what might be the results of fire and brimstone on ancient artefacts. Jericho ought to be even easier because we know where that is, and evidence of ruined walls might still be available. But there are huge problems with this approach.

- It isn't always easy to locate the exact site. Old Testament Jericho is some way to the north of the modern city, for example. In other cases we can only guess at whether a site we have identified corresponds to the biblical one in which we are interested. A city called Ai also forms part of Joshua's story about the conquest of Canaan (Joshua 8). According to Joshua 8.28, 'Joshua burned Ai to the ground and left it the desolate ruined mound it remains to this day.' In fact the name Ai means 'ruin'. The fairly detailed description of the location of this city has led some archaeologists to think they've found it, but uncertainty remains.

- Then there are technical problems to do with the archaeology itself, which is far from straightforward.
- A more serious problem however is that the evidence the biblical archaeologists sought is not being found, and indeed, contradictory evidence *is* being found. Dame Kathleen Kenyon's excavations at Jericho in the 1950s concluded that Jericho was probably uninhabited at the time when the Bible account describes it as a substantial city. American excavations at the supposed site of Ai have shown that that city had lain in ruins since around 2300 BCE – a thousand years before the accepted date of the setting of the biblical account.

These are problems for those who believe this kind of enquiry is fruitful, but the vast majority of scholars disagree about that, casting doubt on the credibility of the enterprise from the outset. That is not to say that archaeology has nothing to offer, and indeed there has been a robust defence of its contribution in the face of the assault, as it is seen, by the so-called reductionists (see especially Dever 2001, 2003). Modern archaeology works hand in hand with sociology, not to prove or disprove the factual accuracy of biblical texts, but to try to piece together what kind of society Israel was, how it emerged, and how it was organized. From the evidence of cultural change (types of pottery used, for example) and population movement (quantity of material found, for example), data is produced. This data is then interpreted in the light of models which have emerged from studies of ancient and modern societies. In turn this provides working hypotheses about the nature of actual historical Israel.

The last forty years have seen the social sciences play a much larger part in Old Testament study. One problem which has been addressed by this kind of study is how Israel emerged in Palestine. The biblical account tells a story of ethnically related slaves miraculously freed from slavery in Egypt, who cross the Sinai Peninsula (with important events and theophanies *en route* at a mountain), and who take the land of Canaan by force. There are both practical and ethical reasons for suspecting this account. No archaeological evidence has emerged in Sinai to support it. There are huge difficulties in piecing together a coherent route for this so-called Exodus. Excavations at the place where the party is described as having spent most time, Kadesh Barnea, have delivered nothing. There is some debate about how to inter-pret the phrase in Exodus 12.37 which describes how many people left with Moses, but taken at its usual face value of 600,000, the resulting movement is quite unimaginable. Marching 25 abreast, it has been estimated that the column would be almost 200 miles long, and that the leaders would have reached modern-day Mount Sinai before the back-markers had left Egypt (Mendenhall 2001, p. 52).

Modern ethical concern is expressed at what this account actually seems to say about God. It describes a God who is apparently quite happy to see wide-scale genocide in order to protect and maintain a people he has chosen quite capriciously. To modern and especially western readers, this arouses far too many of the inherited guilt feelings about their colonial and imperial past, to be comfortable.

Reflection on text

Read Joshua 8.18–29. If you read this as an account of some modern military campaign what would your reaction be? Could something like this ever be justified? How might someone from a faith community come to terms with this kind of writing, do you think?

Even the Bible's special pleading that the indigenous peoples were evil, under-standably cuts little ice. However, it was being claimed as late as the 1930s that the archaeological evidence supported the biblical record (Albright 1939). This was contested by Albrecht Alt. His theory was that the land was settled as a result of pastoral nomadic movement rather than by bloody con-quest. The theory was first propounded in the 1920s (though it is still cur-rent: see for example Finkelstein 1988) and depends on the then current view of human progress. Simply put, this says that humans will naturally progress from being nomads, to being settled peasant farmers and eventually to being urban dwellers. This was contested in a paper, often taken as the modern starting-point of serious sociological study of the Old Testament, entitled 'The Hebrew conquest of Palestine' (Mendenhall 1962). In this essay Mendenhall argues against the accepted 'conquest' model of how Israel emerged in Palestine and the model set out by Albrecht Alt. He argues that this does not take the social scientific evidence seriously enough. His view is that disenfranchised people already resident in Canaan became associated with slaves fleeing from Egypt who carried with them the story of a liberating God Yahweh. These people participated in a kind of 'Peasants' Revolt' which was ultimately successful. The emergent state took the name Israel.

A further work in this area is one of the most influential in Old Testament study in the past fifty years, Norman Gottwald's *The Tribes of Yahweh* (1979). What he and others have been interested in is: What was the unifying factor in this newly emerging Israel within Palestine? What made Israel Israel? Again the biblical account includes a saga-like story which traces the eventual unity of Israel back hundreds of years to patriarchal ancestors like Abraham and Jacob (whose name was changed to Israel). According to this account Israel was an ethnically related group who were all slaves in Egypt and who all entered Canaan from the east across the Jordan. Gottwald's magisterial sociological study, building on the insights of those who contested the biblical account of the settlement, reached different conclusions. What gave Israel its unity was not blood-kinship, ethnic heritage, common cultural practice or shared economic interests, but rather an ideology, the ideology provided by the religion of Yahweh (Mendenhall 2001, pp. 75ff.).

The three classic models

Conquest – W. F. Albright, early twentieth century. On the basis of archaeological research, this model believes the biblical account to be basically credible.

Peaceful infiltration – Albrecht Alt and Martin Noth, early to mid-twentieth century. A gradual process with occasional skirmishes best fits the biblical traditional evidence.

Social revolution – George Mendenhall and Norman Gottwald, mid- to late twentieth century. 'Israelites' were indigenous Canaanites joined by some refugees from Egypt who brought with them traditions of a liberator God.

Modern sociological and archaeological study of the Old Testament claims to have succeeded in making links between historical Israel and biblical Israel, but these are not in the nature of proofs. They are rather more like echoes or resonances, which suggest some historical authenticity in biblical accounts (as opposed to Davies, Whitelam, etc.) but which also highlight huge areas of theological creativity. Within the text itself it is claimed there are pointers to authenticity of a sort. The fact that Israel includes in its story what might be regarded as a shameful episode of slavery seems to point to a reliable tradition – why else include it? Twelve non-Israelites are named in the book of Joshua, e.g. Rahab (2.6), Debir (10.3). All twelve of these names are attested in non-biblical sources and eleven of them are evidenced in the Late Bronze Age, the time in which the book of Joshua is set. On literary grounds, scholars generally believe that the Song of Deborah in Judges 5 is one of the oldest fragments in the Old Testament, datable probably to the twelfth century BCE. Other ancient literary fragments include the Song of the Sea in Exodus 15. Both poems share information with their accompanying prose accounts (see Meyers 2001, p. 68) perhaps pointing to shared ancient tradition. Judges 5.6 may be an indication of the general upheaval in the eastern Mediterranean area in the Late Bronze Age attested from other sources. In addition, there are a few outstanding pieces of archaeological evidence which do refer to the people or events of the Bible, chief of which is probably the Merneptah Stele.

The stele, or victory inscription, dates from 1208 BCE and includes the lines :

Israel is laid waste, his seed is not;
Hurru is become a widow for Egypt.

It is one of the few pieces of 'hard' evidence for the name Israel from these early times. However, it is not clear whether the hieroglyph for Israel refers to any kind of political, ethnic or social group. Because of this ambiguity, this evidence is used to support conflicting arguments.

What then can be said in answer to the question at the head of this chapter?

1. Apart from among the most conservative readers there is widespread agreement that the Old Testament should not be read as a 'record of fact'.
2. The main debate at present is between those who deny any link between 'historical Israel' and 'biblical Israel' on the one hand; and on the other, those who want to argue that even texts written centuries after the events they purport to describe, do include ancient traditions.
3. The discipline of archaeology appears for all practical purposes to regard the Bible not as a privileged account of truth but rather as a 'cultural artefact' like anything else which can be unearthed and needs to be explained and related to culture (see Carter 2001, p. 52).
4. The discipline of sociology has confirmed some aspects of biblical authenticity while highlighting those elements of the Old Testament account which rely on theological creativity. Those elements include large parts of the Exodus, Conquest and Settlement traditions as well as (as we shall see in due course) elements related to the period when Israel was ruled by kings.
5. There is a considerable body of scholars who would argue that the reson-ances between the archaeological and sociological conclusions, and the Old Testament, point to an important grounding of the account in the real world. The Old Testament world was a real and not a fantasy world; and Israel was part of a much larger world.

Carol Meyers' succinct summary would appeal to many. The Old Testa-ment is 'a mixture of fictional imagination and historical memory brought together for ideological purposes' (Meyers 2001, p. 67). The pressing ques-tion almost everyone would agree is not, 'Did it happen?' but rather, 'Why on earth did they tell their story like that?' And that is the question with which we shall be primarily concerned. But first, how does the story go?

CHAPTER 5 SUMMARY

What is this chapter about?

This chapter, the final introductory chapter before we embark on an exploration of the text and contents of the Old Testament, picks up the concept of canon and asks, in the light of all we have learned about the debate around how to read the Old Testament properly: Is there an identifiable theme, or series of themes, with which the reader can work? The chapter refers to the work of three important writers from the middle of the twentieth century onwards who have responded to this question in different ways.

What books are referred to?

The works of Gerhard von Rad are referred to generally. For our purposes his most important works are *Old Testament Theology* (London: SCM Press, vol. 1 1962, vol. 2 1965. Reference is made to Childs' work, for which see the bibliography to Chapter 3. To the work of Brueggemann already cited we can add: Patrick D. Miller (ed.), *Old Testament Theology: Essays on Structure, Theme and Text* (Minneapolis: Fortress Press, 1992). Reference is also made to the following:

Rex Mason, *Propaganda and Subversion in the Old Testament* (London: SPCK, 1997); Erhard Gerstenberger, *Theologies in the Old Testament* (Edinburgh: T & T Clark, 2002), David Clines, *The Theme of the Pentateuch* (Sheffield: Sheffield Academic Press, 1979/1996).

What other books would be helpful?

This is an exhaustive list at this stage.

How is the chapter organized?

The main topics are these: canon revisited; where did scholarship go after Eichrodt? the work of von Rad; the contribution of Childs; Brueggemann as an example of a contemporary writer.

What should I be able to do by the end of this chapter?

Recount the major landmarks in Old Testament study, and major developments in the understanding of how to read the text over the past hundred years or so to the present time.

Be equipped to begin to read the text itself, judiciously.

5

What is the Old Testament About?

If someone were to commend a book to you that you hadn't previously heard of or read, what would be your first question to them? In all likelihood it would be, 'Well what's it about then?' In answer to that question you might expect (depending on the book) to hear something about its setting (it's about the wars between Greece and Turkey); its main characters (it's about these two star-crossed lovers Cathy and Heathcliff); or about the plot (it's about what happens when a child is brought up by fanatically religious foster-parents). As we saw in Chapter 1, the history of scholarship in relation to the question 'What is the Old Testament about?' varies between the periods when scholars thought it was an irrelevant question, and those where they thought it was relevant as a question but disagreed about the answer.

Reflection on experience

Think of any book you know well and try to write in a couple of sentences an answer to the question 'What's it about?' What kind of answer have you given? What did you need to know to give the answer? Think about the kinds of things you might need to know about the Old Testament in order to answer the question in relation to those writings.

During the nineteenth century when historical critical methods were at the cutting edge, the tendency was to look at the trees rather than the wood. Scholars were fascinated by how the final text was put together and transmitted. They were consumed by the exegesis of small portions of text and gleefully pored over variations in the Hebrew that might result in different translations. They were interested in the findings of archaeology – especially of ancient copies of the Bible books – and particularly interested in the religious life of the wider region. In the early years of the twentieth century the German scholar **Walter Eichrodt** expressed dissatisfaction with the results of this scholarship. He wanted to write about the Old Testament in a holistic way instead of the atomized way of the times. He was concerned that the distinctiveness of the Old Testament was being lost in all the research into ancient Near-Eastern religion. He felt that there was a need for a new approach, which would highlight the significance of these writings for human communities, which the somewhat cold scientific method of the times failed to do. Although he accepted that the Old Testament had a resource value for the objective study of religion, he was convinced that it had more to tell us than that – he believed it had something to say about God to people today, and wanted a study that could access that. Finally he was concerned about how the Old Testament was viewed in relation to the New. Some people saw it simply as a series of predictive prophecies which turned out to be true – in other words interpreting the Old Testament completely in the light of the New. He thought that this was wrong and that the Old Testament deserved to be read on its own terms. Enter Old Testament theology.

Eichrodt's *Theology of the Old Testament* is one of the most important works on the Bible in the twentieth century. It attempted something new. There was no recognized way of doing what he set out to do. The obvious way to write a 'theology' came from dogmatic theology. According to this approach you would set out the main theological categories of Christian doctrine: God, man, sin, redemption and so on, and then ask 'What does the Old Testament say about each of these?' Eichrodt rejected this approach. He considered that it constrained the Old Testament in an artificial way. What he wanted to do was not so much impose a structure from some other discipline, but rather get under the skin of the Old Testament people themselves and to describe religious profession as they experienced and understood it. This aim led to a threefold division in his work: God and Israel, God and World, God and Man; but the fundamental underlying principle, the one big idea, the main storyline, the metanarrative, was for him the idea of **Covenant.**

What this means is that if you were to ask Eichrodt, 'What is the Old Testament about?' his reply would be along these lines. The Old Testament is about an agreement between God and humankind called the Covenant. The books of the Old Testament describe, develop and reflect upon this agreement. They use the agreement as a tool for judging and commentating on human society, and as a means of describing what God is like in this religious understanding. Such a book is a resource for a religious community in that it provides a constitutional understanding of their identity. It might well be considered a promising candidate for the title of 'The Old Testament's Big Idea', or perhaps, 'The Old Testament's Connecting Theme'. But not everyone was convinced.

Large sections of the Old Testament (the Wisdom literature, for example) do not seem to have it as a central theme, to say the least. Others accuse Eichrodt of being too verbose: 'I think it no exaggeration to say that Eichrodt's work might be condensed by as much as one third and not lose anything essential' (Gottwald 1979, p. 45). Also, there are several 'editions' of the Covenant and they differ from each other markedly in some respects. For example: the covenant made on Sinai (Exodus 20—24) is made with the people of Israel, and maintains a popular appeal through its championing of the claims of justice. The covenant described in 2 Samuel 7 is made with the king of Israel, rather than the people, and in effect gives him *carte blanche* to act under the protection of God. The covenant with Noah (Genesis 9.8–17) is of a different order altogether as a covenant made with all humankind, including a promise to sustain life on earth.

Reflection on text

Read Exodus 24.3–8, and then 2 Samuel 7.8–16. Both of these passages describe agreements or covenants made between God and humankind. Make a list of the differences you see between them. What do they have in common? Which is the longer list?

Eichrodt's critics say that he does not take enough account of these differences. But the most telling criticism is that Eichrodt falls prey to his own accusation against others, in that he imposes a solution which does not in fact come naturally from the text. Who is to say that there is one big idea contained within the text? Eichrodt assumes that he can find one and stands accused of manipulating the concept of covenant to suit his purposes. It is one thing to say that we need to find some organizing principle to help us through the text. It is quite another to say that the text itself demands or contains this, or that it is in any sense a unity.

The main critic along these lines was **Gerhard von Rad**. He believed that what the text of the Old Testament yielded was not so much a big idea as a dynamic; and he thought that the way to access that dynamic was through the creeds of the faithful of Israel. In this way he hoped truly to arrive at a theology that derived genuinely from the text itself. The kind of texts that interested him were Deuteronomy 6.20–4, 26.5b–10; Joshua 24.2b–13; Psalm 136; Nehemiah 9.6ff., especially vv. 9ff.

Reflection on text

Read Deuteronomy 6.20–4. This passage is set to be recounted in a particular formal setting, perhaps in the same kind of way that congregations recite particular passages together in modern church services. What do you think is 'religious' about this account? What does your answer tell you about the understanding of God which underlies it?

What these passages describe is the people of Israel's understanding of salvation. Their first experience of God is of a God who acts to save them from actual harm. The key experience through which they describe the beginnings of their faith is one in which God acts in the political sphere to liberate them. The characteristic 'shape' of the story runs thus: there is need; people call out of need; God hears and acts; he saves; the saved respond (see for example Exodus 2.23f.). The interpretation of history along these lines is called salvation history, and if you had asked von Rad what the Old Testament is about he might well have replied 'salvation history, and the God who acts'. In other words, the Old Testament is about a dynamic and involved God who liberates his people and intervenes in their lives and political processes.

Such a book is a resource for a religious community in that each generation is invited afresh to consider what this original story or history of salvation means in their context. This view too has its critics. Again, the distribution of these credal texts is patchy. Again there are variations in the meaning of salvation. If von Rad were searching for what is unique about the Old Testament, then this does not fit the bill because other cultures have gods who act in history to rescue their followers. Some think he misunderstood the Hebrew concept of time. Others have considered that the relation between salvation history and real history in von Rad's thinking is unclear. What really happened?

Despite the criticisms these were the two major attempts at a theology of the Old Testament during the first sixty years or so of the twentieth century (for others see the reading list in the chapter summary). Most writers found it necessary to refer to them. Some developed their ideas. Westermann was particularly interested in how salvation was understood once the people had settled and no longer needed to be saved from physical danger. He believed that in settled times 'blessing' came to be the counterpart of 'salvation'. This was the constant understanding of God's continuing interest and presence. Along with blessing comes the idea of curse and judgement. Salvation comes to have a more moral force. People are saved not so much from danger as from 'the enemy within' – sin. Salvation is no longer accomplished through parting seas and effecting escape from oppression, but rather through forgiveness. Others believed that an impasse had been reached. 'The comprehensive designs of Walther Eichrodt and Gerhard von Rad are now found wanting and we must find a new shape' (Brueggemann 1992, p. 1).

One attempt to do something new came from an American scholar, **Brevard S. Childs**. He introduced the concept of 'canonical criticism'. This title points us towards what is novel in his approach. He believes that we ought to concentrate less on how the text was produced and more on how it was received, and especially how it was formed into a canon of scripture by the Christian church. 'Much of the confusion in the history of Old Testament theology derives from the reluctance to recognize that it is a Christian enterprise' (Childs 1985, p. 8). He puts much stress on the church's role, and on the relationship between the Old and New Testaments.

Canon

The 'canon of scripture' is a technical term which describes the church's influence in deciding which writings, from those available, are going to be regarded as Holy Scripture in a special sense. This is something readers often take for granted and give little thought to, but in the case of both Old and New Testaments conscious decisions were taken at various stages to include some works and exclude others in order to form the Christian Bible, or the Hebrew scriptures, the TaNaK. The word 'canon' means 'yardstick', the means by which a proper pace is measured for marching soldiers. The canon of scripture is meant to be the foundation documents of faith which are reliable yardsticks – reliable points of reference for adherents of the faith. We have already seen how the canon of the Old Testament developed over hundreds of years in a threefold way, with the final 'signing-off' at the Council of Jamnia, a council of Pharisees, in the last decade of the first century CE. There is a collection of apocrypha and pseudipigrapha available in English translation. Some of those books are accepted as canonical, with varying degrees of authority by different Christian churches. There is also an extensive collection of apocryphal books to accompany the New Testament, some of which were regarded as Holy Writ by some churches from early times, but are no longer part of Christian Bibles. The final decision as to what was regarded as the New Testament was not made until 397 CE, almost 400 hundred years after the events the New Testament describes.

He was of course quite right to stress that 'Old Testament' is a Christian term and that it presupposes a 'New' Testament – Jewish scholars do not write Old Testament theologies. However, scholars have been cautious to place as much reliance on the canonical process as does Childs. After all this was a very haphazard, and to some extent undocumented, process which took place over centuries, and it is possible from our modern standpoint to credit it with a coherence it does not deserve. Others have found his work confusing, opinionated and offering little that is new. It does raise interesting questions about the church's ownership of the scriptures, and reminds us that these texts are not naive, and that they are consciously deployed to win converts, specifically to Christianity. Childs could be said to have two answers to the question 'What is the Old Testament about?' One is to say, well you'll only understand that if you read the New Testament as well, and remember all the time that this is the edited version of a lot of texts to produce, in its entirety, the book of the church. The other answer is more pedestrian. It is that the Old Testament describes what Childs calls two kinds of life: life under threat and life under promise.

Indeed it has been a feature of more recent attempts to produce a theology of the Old Testament, that their authors present us with a set of such antitheses, or at least bipolar possibilities. So we have schemes based on threat and promise (Childs), blessing and deliverance (Westermann) propaganda and subversion (Mason). One of the more interesting schemes is that of **Walter Brueggemann.** On the one hand he sees the Old Testament as in some way authorizing the royal and priestly establishment, in the same way that other ancient societies attempt to achieve and authenticate structures for maintaining peace and order. He calls this the 'legitimization of structure', and says it is not unique. In tension with this is another strand in the texts, which speaks out on behalf of those oppressed by the very establishment that has been legitimized. This he calls the Old Testament's 'embrace of pain'. The unresolved tension of these two reflects the ambivalence of human existence under God and is a unique feature. Rex Mason's division of the material into that which acts as royal/priestly propaganda, and that which is prophetically subversive (Mason 1997) explores the same area.

The idea is this. Imagine a foreign head of state visiting Britain. The Government wishes to woo him or her, perhaps with a view to lucrative trade deals. However the human rights record of this state is appalling. One evening the head of state is the guest at a banquet in Buckingham Palace. Representatives of the church are present at this state occasion, but on their way into the palace are met by crowds of protestors from Christian organizations, highlighting the human rights abuse. There is a real tension involved in recognizing that both the church leaders and the protestors are on the same side. Paul Oestreicher, a peace activist Christian priest, describes this tension well as, accidentally, he finds himself sharing a hotel room with a military chaplain (Oestreicher 1986, p. 11). There is a tension between those who are Christians because the church has strong moral codes, supports law and order, encourages 'family values', and offers forgiveness for individuals' sin, on the one hand; and those who are Christians because they believe the church is inclusive, honouring people who are perceived as different (gays, ethnic minorities, the disabled, the mentally ill, for example) and assuring them of equality in the sight of God; being the voice for the poor and un-heard, and the best hope of justice for the oppressed. In other words this is a tension we can recognize, and if Brueggemann is correct, this recognition gives us a new interest (in the technical sense of 'stake') in how the Bible texts deal with this. It becomes our story. It would probably take Bruegge-mann a book at least to answer the question 'What is the Old Testament about?' but I guess his most succinct answer might be to point us to the recognizable tensions of living as a member of a faith community in today's world, and say, 'It's about that.'

What do we need to remember from this brief summary?

1. The search for a theology of the Old Testament was one response to fears that scholarship was missing the big picture.
2. For most of the twentieth century the task was carried out mainly by Christians.
3. In the early stages there was an assumption about the unity of the Old Testament, and an assumption that it did in fact have a theme.
4. There is a difference between claiming to have found a unifying theme demanded by the text itself, i.e. *identifying* the Old Testament's implicit theology, on the one hand; and searching for or *creating* some modern organizational principle that might help us access the texts from our standpoint, on the other.
5. In the later stages of the last century the earlier assumptions were chal-lenged. Unifying principles developed into bipolar tensions, and the Christian privilege was questioned.
6. These later stages coincided both with the development of literary criticism and with the cultural shift towards postmodernism.

Another way of describing what a particular book is about might be in terms of the motives which you the reader perceive behind the writing, or in terms of the literary strategy of the book. So, for example, you might answer a question about some book by saying, 'It's an attempt to persuade us that there were humane slave-owners.' Or you might say of another, 'It's a satire about political power in the twentieth century'; or again about a third, 'It's a surreal and ironic perspective on white South Africa before apartheid ended.' Further questions would be in order in each case. 'How does it persuade us about the slave-owners? What rhetorical devices does it use?' Or, 'What does the satire refer to?' Or again, 'How does the irony operate?' In each of these cases we would be saying in effect: on the surface this book is about such and such a thing, but actually there's more to it than that, there's something under the surface. To describe what the book is about would then be to describe the 'hidden' motive. This is the approach of literary critics of the Old Testament. And a pretty important approach it is too. If a piece of work is meant to be satirical or ironic and we read it in a 'flat' literal way, we have misunderstood it. If there's a motive underlying the writing that has determined the style and shape of the piece and we take it at face value then we have been naive in our reading. As we have noted, one movement among critics has been to concentrate more on the later part of the Old Testament period, post-exilic times, when the text reached its final form. And questions have been asked about why it was presented in this way, in order to reach a different kind of answer as to what it's about.

One of the earliest literary critics to address this kind of issue was **David Clines.** *The Theme of the Pentateuch* was first published in the 1970s but recently reprinted as a classic critical piece. This is, in effect, an extended essay, which asks whether the Pentateuch has a theme. No-one had asked the question before in this way. The classic answer (see Chapter 6) was that of Martin Noth, that there were several themes. On the surface this is demonstrably true, but Clines wants to know if there is a deeper underlying motive. After all, this collection, the end-product of a long process of tradition perhaps, is a very sophisticated series of documents, consciously produced. Why was it published in this form? What made it a relevant publication in its time? Clines' answer is in two parts. First, he does identify a theme. That theme is about unfulfilled or partially fulfilled promise. Second, and importantly as it turned out for future scholarship, he put forward the view that although the story told was about the Exodus, the context in which it was told was the aftermath of the Exile. The story of partially fulfilled promise was one that was very relevant to the returning exiles, once again on the brink of the promised land. If he was right, then we must read the Exodus accounts in a different, less naive, way. It may well be that on the surface they are about the Exodus, but in a very important way, they are about the experience of exile.

The technical term for reading a text in a way which expects that it might be about something other than what it seems to be about, is **the hermeneutic of suspicion**. The term derives from sociology, where it is a tool for those trying to discern where power lies. Reading a text in this way one asks, 'To whose advantage is it to present the story thus? Who is disadvantaged or silenced by presenting it thus?' In the Old Testament for example, we very rarely hear the voice of women. In recorded history generally we rarely hear the voice of the poor, and so on. A suspicious reading of the Old Testament might lead us to believe, among other things, that it is about an attempt to define a post-exilic religious community using pre-exilic traditions to tell a story about Israel's history which makes the events of the Exodus the key events for understanding what is distinctive in the community eight or nine hundred years later. It's about an exilic people telling a story to define who they are, about an exodus.

Reflection on text

Read Exodus 20.1–17. This is the familiar list of ten words (or ten commandments). Pursuing his hermeneutic of suspicion, David Clines asks: In whose interest are they written? For example, the commandment not to steal is clearly in the interests of people who own property. Look through the list and see what conclusions you come to. Would you agree with Clines that they are written in the interests of 'a balding Israelite urban male with a mid-life crisis and a weight problem, in danger of losing his faith' (Clines 1995, p. 34)?

Now, these attempts to answer the question that heads the chapter are not mutually exclusive. They are quite mixable and matchable. Also, read in conjunction with the last chapter, it is possible to give more or less credence to the integrity of traditional material. So it is possible to believe that the whole thing is a fiction, composed in the post-exilic period, describing something that had no connection with history at all. It is also possible to hold that the post-exilic writers did depend on genuine traditions, and that these traditions did have a theological charge within them, about a covenant, or about a God who acts and saves or both. Postmodern culture gives us permission to think that there may be lots of theologies contained in this volume and not just one (see for example Gerstenberger 2002). It gives us permission to reach our own view, and to test the effect the texts have on us.

And so we are ready to embark on the adventure of Old Testament reading. We can begin to enter the world of sex, glamour, violence, corruption, celebrity, media, and human drama, which it contains. We do so knowing that one of the main characters in this drama is God, which makes it special and different; and that part of the difference is that millions of people from faith communities throughout the world, now and throughout history, have lived their lives in a faith that has an intimate connection with what we are reading. To that extent it deserves respect. But no longer, in the academy at least, does it have privilege.

CHAPTER 6 SUMMARY

What is this chapter about?

We begin our survey of the text of the Old Testament with an overview of the Pentateuch, concentrating on the earliest traditions of J and E, and thus focusing particularly on Genesis and Exodus.

What books are referred to?

The following new books are referred to: G. E. Mendenhall, *Law and Covenant in Israel and the Ancient Near East* (Pittsburgh: Biblical Colloquium, 1955), a ground-breaking work whose arguments are carried forward in a number of more recent works by Mendenhall, including Mendenhall (2001); David Clines, *Interested Parties* (Sheffield: Sheffield Academic Press, 1995); James Cone, *God of the Oppressed* (London: SPCK, 1977); A. R. Ceresko, *Introduction to the Old Testament: A Liberation Perspective* (London: Geoffrey Chapman, 1992); and Paula Gooder, *The Pentateuch: A Story of Beginnings* (London: Continuum, 2000). (This last book is particularly recommended for those who want to dig deeper. It also contains further helpful bibliography.)

What other books would be helpful?

For those who want to explore the Liberation perspective, a good starting-point to get a taster of what's around is: Norman Gottwald and Richard Horsley (eds), *The Bible and Liberation* (London: SPCK, 1993). For those who would like an update on the Documentary Thesis discussion, there is a useful article by Gordon Wenham, entitled 'Pondering the Pentateuch', in David Baker and Bill Arnold (eds), *The Face of Old Testament Studies* (Leicester: IVP, 1999).

How is the chapter organized?

The main topics are as follows: Genesis, Exodus, Covenant. Then, other themes in the Pentateuch, including: Liberation, Promise and Fulfilment, and Land.

What should I be able to do by the end of this chapter?

Outline the main themes of the Pentateuch.

Outline the contents of Genesis and Exodus.

Evaluate some critical discussion around these books.

6

In the Beginning

Reflection on experience

Are you at all familiar with any part of the first five books of the Old Testament? If not, read on, but if you are, think for a moment about the passages you are familiar with. What kind of passages are they? In what context did you come to know them? If you are a member of a faith community, have they played any part in defining the life of that community for you?

Despite credible claims from other parts of the literature, Genesis is not a bad place to start to read the Old Testament. When you do so, you need to remember what we have already noticed:

- That the first five books of the Old Testament form one discrete section, the Pentateuch;
- That source critics have identified four main sources for the work as a whole;
- That form critics have identified that even these four sources are made up of smaller units of different kinds of material including sagas, poems, narrative and songs;
- That latterly, critics like David Clines (1979) have tried to identify one consistent theme for the Pentateuch, and suggested that that theme is partially fulfilled/partially unfulfilled promise.

That all being said, it is important not to feel too hemmed in by all that. It would be quite wrong to read each few verses wondering, 'Is this a saga or a legend?' or 'Is this J or P?' as if that were all there were to gaining a full understanding. We need a bit more space than that to read with enjoyment, and indeed the Pentateuch can be an enjoyable read. Genesis is probably the most readable book of the five. This is because it begins with some very striking universal images, and continues with some of the liveliest narrative. The story of Joseph comes from this book, and that has made it in a successful musical adaptation: *Joseph and His Amazing Technicolour Dreamcoat*. Exodus is not far behind, with its stirring stories of liberation. The least attractive is probably Numbers. Even the author's aunty would have been hard pressed to plough through to the end. Leviticus is an acquired taste, and like Deuteronomy becomes more interesting when we know why it was written (see Chapter 7). There is disagreement, as we have seen, about how reliable the alleged oldest sources are historically, but there is common acceptance that the Pentateuch does introduce us to very important theological ideas and themes which will recur throughout the Old and indeed New Testaments.

The whole thing begins with eleven chapters that deal with universal themes, as opposed to the story of the people of Israel in particular. Older commentators of say the nineteenth century, reflecting the concerns of their day, believed that these chapters were evidence in the case between religion and science. A famous Archbishop of Armagh even determined the date of Creation as 4004 BCE on the basis of his reading of the texts! Scholars of the so-called History of Religions School, on the other hand, were busy finding links between the stories of creation and flood in Genesis 1—11, and similar stories from other ancient civilizations, and deciding what if any link there was between them. Although this all seems very quaint to us now, it is perhaps worth remembering that there are places in the world where religious ideas about creation are still an issue. In some states of America it is still illegal to teach anything other about the creation of the world than that it happened in seven days. According to the travel writer Bill Bryson, this is evidence not so much that we were descended from apes, as that we have been overtaken by them.

The kinds of questions that are raised nowadays in the scholarly community at least, in relation to these texts, are rather different. The two creation accounts in Genesis 1.1—2.3, and Genesis 2.4—3.24 are read now in relation to the findings of source critics, that they come from different authors in different periods. Genesis 1 is the later, post-exilic writing. Genesis 2 and 3 comes from the earlier JE traditions. Although this might seem strange, a moment's thought shows how this has happened. The later writers want to put their final stamp on the story, and so contribute the introduction. Read against the supposed historical backgrounds, what we see is the JE tradition giving us a picture of humankind that derives from the confident times when Israel was a sovereign nation at peace. Man is created first in all creation and he is in charge. He even names the animals (and in Hebrew to give someone or something a name is to demonstrate power over it). There seems to be nothing he cannot do, with his close and assured relationship with God. The P tradition comes from the period where all this optimism has disappeared. The Exile has happened, and God seems far away. In this account humankind is created last (man and woman together). Humankind comes almost as a guest to an already created world, trying to discern its rules and order, tentatively beginning to understand the interconnectedness of creation of which humankind is but one part. The JE traditions are brash and confident. The P tradition is comparatively pacifist and concerned with wholeness. The aim of Genesis 1, on this reading, is to present a picture of a sacred society with delicate balances and interdependence, in which the humans' responsibility is to exercise pastoral care. For the P writers, the issues are not about how to exercise power and run a nation-state. They are about how to live in the world in the awareness of the presence and care of a universal God.

These early chapters are not then about how the world was created, but rather about the intentions and destiny of creation, and the place of human-kind in it all. To an extent there is a clash with Darwinism, but not the one usually fought over. The theory of evolution and its scientific humanist religious counterpart believes that there is continual progress in creation, and that in principle human beings may reach perfection. The biblical view, whether from JE or P, is more 'realistic' in that it presupposes a fall from perfection. The main question of the first eleven chapters then becomes a choice between two ways of understanding human destiny in the world. Option A is the pessimistic view, that God's good creation will inevitably be subverted by corrupt humankind. Option B is the more optimistic view that inevitably God's grace will overcome human evil. What we see in these chapters is a series of scenarios in which these options are presented, sometimes in a very radical way. By the end of chapter 11 we are still not sure what the answer is, but we are at least sure that this is the main issue. And in a sense it is the questions raised by this issue that the Bible as a whole grapples with.

After the creation sequences in Genesis 1—3, there are three other main scenarios. The first is the story of Cain and Abel in Genesis 4. It has been standard in interpretation of this passage to try to 'get God off the hook' by suggesting all kinds of reasons why he may have been justified in refusing Cain's sacrifice and accepting Abel's. However, this really misses the point. This is a description of life as it is experienced, in which there seems to be no justifiable reason for lots of things that happen, and in which, as it were, human beings seem to be, all too often, the victims of capricious gods. The next scenario is the series of flood stories. Again there are two sources with different agendas. The P part of the story includes the covenant between God and Noah (Genesis 9.1–17) in which God promises to maintain life on earth. In Genesis 10 and 11 we then have two different estimates of human diversity. The P conclusion is that this is a consequence of God's good intentions in creation (chapter 10). The JE conclusion is that different languages and cultures are related to disobedience and human ambition. It is possible to make the case for either conclusion from the reader's own experience and it is our interest in the resolution of these questions as much as in the artistry of the writing that maintains our attention.

Reflection on text

Read Genesis 11.1–9. Older commentators saw passages like these as offering explanations of how various tribes and nations came into being. More recent readings see something here of greater theological depth about diversity in human society. They key item for reflection revolves around the difference between unity and scattering. Chapter 10 describes scattering in a very positive way – what has been called an ecumenical vision – but chapter 11 sees it as a punishment for a people who regard unity in an exclusive way, and a means of exercising power inappropriately. What application do you think this passage has to today's society? Has it anything to contribute, for example, to debates about racism, tolerance of difference, religious ecumenism?

Most of the rest of the book of Genesis comes from the JE tradition, and takes the form of sagas about the nation of Israel's supposed ancestors. Little evidence exists to confirm or deny the historicity of these sagas but that is not the real issue. It is through these stories that the character of God begins to unfold in the social and political sphere, and the nature of the particular relationship that humans can have with God in order to make life meaningful and bearable begins to emerge. In particular we begin to anticipate a special relationship based on God's promise to these people that they will have progeny (Genesis 12.2f.; 15.5) a land of their own (15.7) and an ongoing special relationship. (The P account in Genesis 17.1–8 is the most succinct summary.) As the story is told, it concerns Abraham, his son Isaac, Isaac's son Jacob who is renamed Israel, and in turn, his twelve sons. A more complete 'novel' deals with the adventures of one of these sons, Joseph, and incidentally locates the family group of Israel within Egypt. This location is important in the next stage of the story.

At the beginning of the book of Exodus some important new features are introduced.

- For the first time (Exodus 2.23–5), God relates to the community of Israel and not just to favoured individuals. This new relationship is born of the suffering of the people.
- We are introduced to the idea that God works through a specific human agent as liberator and redeemer. This agent is Moses.
- (Exodus 3.14) God reveals his name YHWH, which is not so much a revelation as a joke. In Hebrew thought, to know someone's name is to have power over them, so in a special sense it is impossible to know God's name since, if you did, he would no longer be God. It is incompatible with the idea of God that you can define him, because that would be to limit him – a constant human religious ambition that is

consistently resisted in the tradition. Hence we are teased into thinking we are going to learn God's name (just as in the Tower of Babel story we think we might build something which reaches up to the heavens; or in the creation story we are teased to think that by eating the fruit of the tree of life we can know what God knows) only to learn that the name of God is 'I am what I am and I will be what I will be'!

Reflection on text

Read Exodus 2.23–5. This is an important passage, which sets out how the people of Israel understand God as working in relation to them. Look at the verbs in the passage. How well do you think they describe the relation between humankind and God more generally?

Through the agency of Moses, the Israelites are freed from Egyptian oppression and begin their journey through the wilderness toward the promised land of Canaan. Along the way they reach a mountain, variously called Sinai (J and P) or Horeb (E and D), where the special relationship between God and the people is set out and ratified. The remainder of the book of Exodus; the whole of the book of Leviticus, and the book of Numbers up to Numbers 10.10, deal with this so-called Sinai covenant. Numbers 10.11, onwards to the end of that book describe wanderings in the desert on the way to the land. The book of Deuteronomy is set in the plains of Moab as the people prepare to enter the land. To this extent the final version of the Pentateuch offers a coherent narrative. However, it is clear that the importance of the Sinai covenant has prompted writers from a variety of times and circumstances to reflect upon it afresh and add to it. In the popular British TV sitcom *Only Fools and Horses*, a recurring device that the main character Del boy uses when he wants to invoke authority for his decisions, particularly with regard to his younger brother Rodney, is to say 'I remember what our poor mother's dying words were. She said: "always make sure that Rodney . . ."' The audience recognizes this rather devious device for Del to get his own way, for what it is, and it becomes quite comic. Poor old Moses is no less comic as, in similar fashion, generations of writers count him as an ally in their campaigns. Originally, perhaps, he went up the mountain once and came down with the ten words or Decalogue. But as the story now stands, between Exodus 19.3 and Exodus 34.4 he actually goes up at least five times! (19.3; 19.20; 24.9; 24.13 and 34.4). This does point us to the importance of what is described, for the tradition. The Sinai covenant will become one of the most important of biblical ideas.

Here are eight things to know about the Covenant.

1. Actually there are two covenants, or perhaps more accurately, two families of covenant in the Old Testament. The other one is introduced at 2 Samuel 7 (see also 2 Samuel 23.1–5 and Psalm 89) and is often known as the Davidic covenant. The difference between the two is that the Sinai or Mosaic covenant is an agreement between God and the people directly; whereas the Davidic covenant is an agreement between God and the king, favouring the establishment rather than the populace and apparently granting the dynasty the right to rule for ever unconditionally (Psalm 89.19–37). Some scholars see a real tension between the two (e.g. Brueggemann 1992, pp. 1–44; Mason 1997), perhaps even amounting to a defining characteristic of Old Testament theology.

2. Albrecht Alt is responsible for distinguishing between two kinds of law within the Sinai covenant. The ten words or Decalogue he called apodeictic (i.e. straight from God) and these he considered unconditional. Alongside them are casuistic commands which are context-based and derivative.

3. The theological principle that is important in the Covenant is that it is God's initiative. It is the unfolding story of the Pentateuch that humankind is unable of itself to solve its predicament. God sees and God acts. Humans are called to respond. This is part of an interrelated sequence of initiatives, which include God creating and God giving. Each of these initiatives demands human response. The willingness to respond appropriately is counted as obedience, and its opposite, disobedience.

4. A further theological principle follows from Mendenhall's generally accepted proposal that the form of the Covenant mirrors that of treaties between Hittite masters and their vassals. The Covenant is an agreement between unequal partners, between the strong and the weaker.

The point here is that God is portrayed as embarking on this relationship not because he is in some way forced to but because he wants to, though he has no need to do so. In theological terms this is a prime example of God's love and God's grace.

5. The Covenant as a concept is used subsequently in the tradition. Eichrodt believed this was such an important concept that it was possible to describe the whole theology of the Old Testament in terms of it. He was criticized partly on the grounds that it is not evidenced everywhere in the Old Testament – it is more or less absent from the Wisdom writings for example. However, we do see its use in the prophetic writings where the Covenant is used as a measure of Israel's behaviour. In those writings, the Covenant is sometimes more simply formulated, and develops a technical vocabulary of its own, which includes words that are usually translated in English by terms like: constant love, truth, mercy, righteousness, justice, and loving-kindness. So for example Micah 6.8:

> The Lord has told you mortals what is good,
> And what is it that the Lord requires of you:
> Only to act justly, to love loyalty,
> To walk humbly with your God.

6. The covenant ceremony in Exodus 24.3–8 is echoed both in later New Testament tradition at the last supper (specifically at Matthew 26.28; Mark 14.24; and by allusion in John) and in modern Christian holy communion services. Some Christian denominations make covenant an important part of their ecclesiology (i.e. their understanding of what it is to be a church) – so the Methodist Church, for example. This kind of comment would be particularly important to those who might call themselves canonical critics, and who want to see the whole canon of scripture and its subsequent management by the Christian church as the proper context for exegesis.

7. Mendenhall has made the point that 'it would be wrong to look for the profundity of the Decalogue in its *content*' (Mendenhall 2001, p. 60, his italics). In fact the commandments are not strikingly different from other law codes from many times and cultures. Adultery and murder

receive sanction in most societies. Calling the Decalogue the ten *com-mitments* rather than commandments, he suggests that their import-ance is in their context and application, and the extent to which they provide the basis for a shared identity among the people who want to call themselves Israel.

8. The details of the precise way in which Moses is described as having 'received' these commandments are largely seen by scholars as literary and cultural conventions, though as Clines observes this is rarely stated outright. He writes at length on what he sees as a disingenuity among scholars on this point and it is worth quoting him to give a flavour of the kind of problem he sees – a problem of hermeneutics which all Old Testament readers have to solve in some way.

Did God actually speak audible words out of the sky in the Arabian Peninsula in the late second millennium BCE? . . . It will not shock many readers of these pages if I say that I do not believe that any such thing ever happened . . . [but] . . . not a single commentator I have found remarks on this datum of the text, not one confronts the claim of the text with their own personal refusal to accept its ideology. (Clines 1995, pp. 27f.)

He goes on to outline the strategies scholars have adopted, as he sees it, to avoid the question.

Although the Covenant has huge theological importance in the Penta-teuch, there are other theological themes, some of which we have already noted, which tell us something about how God is understood, and how humankind can best live in the world, according to the Old Testament. It is usual for introductions to make reference to Martin Noth's five themes of the Pentateuch. These are actually five stages in the narrative, namely: the promise to the patriarchs, the exodus from Egypt, the wandering in the wilderness, the revelation at Sinai, and the entry into the land. Noth believed that these five were originally distinct traditions, and that the Exodus and Sinai traditions were brought together by the J author. The entry as such is not part of the Pentateuch. Those, like von Rad, who believe that the entry belongs with this collection prefer to speak of a Hexateuch to include the book of Joshua. Those, like Clines, who believe the key theme in the Pentateuch to be *un*-fulfilled promise, believe it is crucial to retain the traditional boundaries. Canonical critics would also take this view.

We shall look at some other themes in the next two chapters that are distinctively associated with either the D or P writers, but it is worth mentioning three themes here.

1. The Exodus account is a prime text for **liberation theology**. This movement, which began not in academies but among oppressed communities, sees in the story of a God who acts to rescue a suffering but faithful community, something of their own story. Von Rad believed that this was how Israel first understood and appreciated God – as a liberator and player in the political arena, and not as creator. He based his belief on what he considered early credal statements from Deuteronomy (e.g. 26.5ff.). At the very least this presents to us a God who *acts* rather than a God who simply *is*, a concept which it is difficult if not impossible, in any case, to convey in the Hebrew language. Liberation theologians go on to see this action of God evident in other parts of the tradition. A couple of quotations make the point.

    There is no knowledge of Yahweh except through his political activity on behalf of the weak and helpless of the land. . . . Theology ceases to be a theology of the Exodus/Sinai tradition when it fails to see Yahweh as unquestionably in control of history, vindicating the weak against the strong. (Cone 1977, p. 65)

    Again and again it has been a story of struggle from oppression, exploitation and injustice. Again and again the God of the Old Testament is recognized as one who has taken sides in that struggle. (Ceresko 1992, p. 303)

2. As has been mentioned, the concept of **promise and fulfilment** is an important part of the biblical dynamic, which we first meet here. This has influenced reading strategies to the extent that for some Christian readers the relation of the Old Testament to the New can be seen in this way. The Old is the promise, the New is the fulfilment. Certainly

some New Testament writers themselves use this strategy as part of their apologetic. For our part it is important to remember that within the Pentateuch the promises are not fulfilled. The land is not entered. It is also useful to remember that for the faithful community of Christians nowadays, the dynamics of hope are still based on unfulfilled or partially fulfilled promises of a new heaven and a new earth. Faith is fed by personal sightings, allusions, hints and suggestions of the presence of God, which give substance to that hope, often in the face of evidence.

3.   The concept of **land** itself is given theological significance by these accounts. The same Hebrew word describes the earth that God created and the land of Israel that he gifted. Both are seen as good, as part of God's design, and as the context for right stewardship and obedience. But when combined with an inalienable right to political statehood in perpetuity, this is a concept which has huge modern repercussions, and which Old Testament scholarship is well aware of.

The Pentateuch is well described as a story of beginnings (Gooder 2000). But it is not a simple story of what once happened. It is a sophisticated account which over centuries has been reworked and added to, in order to continue to give an ongoing sense of cohesion, identity and meaning to all those who consider themselves children of Abraham.

Reflection on text

Read Genesis 17.1–14. This is the keynote P account of the promise to Abraham. As you read it, note the specific promises which God makes. Note also the P insistence on circumcision as the mark of covenant-keeping. Think of this account as being written after the Exile, at a time when Israel had little security, and when it seemed as if all the promises had been broken. Does this alter your view of the passage?

CHAPTER 7 SUMMARY

What is this chapter about?

This chapter is an introduction to one of the main theological strands in the Old Testament, the Deuteronomistic strand, together with a description of the contents of the books in sequence from Deuteronomy through to 2 Kings.

What books are referred to?

No new books are referred to in this chapter.

What other books would be helpful?

Books which will be particularly helpful include:

Mendenhall (2001) and Mills (1999). The latter is specifically about this body of literature and is highly recommended. Those who would like to read a slightly off-beat but entertaining Jewish approach to some of the narrative might read Jonathan Kirsch, *The Harlot by the Side of the Road: Forbidden Tales of the Bible* (London: Rider, 1997). Two commentaries on Deuteronomy also cover the issues and enable further delving. They are, in the Abingdon series, by Walter Brueggemann (Nashville: Abingdon Press, 2001); and in the Interpretation series, by Patrick D. Miller (Louisville: John Knox Press, 1990). Deuteronomy is such a central book in Old Testament interpretation that it 'attracts' commentary. Two other very readable works are G. von Rad, *Deuteronomy* (London: SCM Press, 1966); and R. E. Clements, *God's Chosen People* (London: SCM Press, 1968, also the same author's *Deuteronomy*, 2nd edn (Sheffield: JSOT Press, 1997).

How is the chapter organized?

The chapter begins by defining the material in questions and relating it to the rest of the Old Testament. A discussion on style and themes leads to a description of the contents of the books. Finally there is comment about the changing face of criticism in relation to these works.

What should I be able to do by the end of this chapter?

Describe the contents of the books from Deuteronomy to 2 Kings.

Recognize the current critical issues, and relate them to the critical approaches work already done.

Relate the main theological themes of this writing.

7

Terrorists or Visionaries? The Contribution of D

Imagine (if you can) living in a society in which religion doesn't have much clout. There is still a definite religious presence, bearing witness to an historic association between society and religion that has long since ceased to have much substance. Nevertheless, some public holidays still coincide with religious festivals, and the language of religion is still evident and publicly recognized. You are aware that there are lots of religious ceremonies carried out in a variety of ways all over the place by specially designated people, but they play little part in public life. There is anecdotal evidence that it was not always thus, and that there were times when religion played a vital part in the life of the nation, but these, people say, are more modern times. They are also anxious times for society. The international situation is precarious and there is some domestic disquiet. You look in vain for good news on any front. There are rumours of political intrigue. And then something quite unexpected happens. A new king arrives and allies himself with an emerging group of politico-religious radicals. Their fundamental message harks back to earlier religious heroes whose words they quote. They advocate a new partnership between religion and state and they initiate a radical new policy with regard to religion, restricting public religious practice to one centre of excellence, and closing down the rest. They insist that the present situation in the nation will only be improved with a new devotion to the religion once espoused (apparently) by the nation long ago. To this end a radical re-education programme is initiated, based in homes rather than religious buildings, and centred on teaching in the context of family occasions. A book is produced to both justify and resource the new programme and its underlying principles. How would you react? Would you regard these people as an exciting new prospect for the nation, breaking free of the vicious circles and dead ends that life had seemed to offer hitherto; or would you regard them as fundamentalist fanatics, driven and dangerous? That is still the choice on offer, in effect, for readers of Deuteronomy.

Reflection on experience

Look again at the scenario outlined above. Are any parts of it recognizable to you? If you were to make comparisons between that scenario and your own experience, what events from your country's situation would you choose? A basic issue throughout this discussion of the Deuteronomic writers will be the relationship between 'church' and 'state'. Is this something you have a view on? At the end of the chapter revisit this question and see if it has been focused for you in any way.

Scholars have generally followed Martin Noth in regarding the books from Joshua to 2 Kings as coming from the same milieu as Deuteronomy. Hence their designation as the Deuteronomistic History, or D history. In considering the D writers, we shall be looking at all these works. Perhaps the first thing to do is to see how they are connected to other parts of the Old Testament.

- Traditionally, there is a connection with King Josiah. 2 Kings 22.1—23.30 offers a glowing report of Josiah's reign. During his time a new law scroll was 'discovered' by workmen in the Temple (22.8–13) which is adopted by Josiah. This is usually identified as the book of Deuteronomy.
- There is an important connection with the Exile. The time of writing coincides with the final years before exile and the early years of that exile. The end of the D history is, in effect, the end of the story of Israel as a sovereign nation.

- There is a connection with the prophets. The message of the D devotees bears striking resemblance to those of the prophets of the eighth century BCE. Both make the Covenant the basis of their theology. Both have an interest in the relation between religion and society. Both are critical of society in similar ways. It is worth remembering that although Deuteronomy is part of the Torah section of the Old Testament, the books from Joshua to 2 Kings are part of the Prophets section. In fact they have the special designation 'Former Prophets'. A further link is with the prophets of the late seventh century, and especially Jeremiah, who was one of the D reformers. Jeremiah's story is a movingly tragic one as it is portrayed. His father was the overseer of one of the outlying shrines which the D people were responsible for shutting down, thus putting Jeremiah at odds with his own family, as a result of which he is separated from them.

- There is a connection with the Pentateuch. D is one of the four sources of the Pentateuch. However, it is different from the other three, in that it does not intertwine with them to produce a composite narrative, but rather sets out a discrete independent account which unashamedly is presented as an update. Only the D histories offer an account of the conquest of Canaan and the settlement in the land. The fact that these writings come from a group with such an overt theological agenda is one of the reasons why scholars are hesitant to treat them as a record of events.

- There is a connection with the books of Chronicles, Ezra and Nehemiah. These books also tell the story of Israel from the beginnings of monarchy to the end of the Exile, using the D histories as a source. They also recount the post-exilic return. These were, however, written after the Exile and have a different agenda.

The D histories are essentially written in the face of the experience of exile to try to answer the question, 'How could God let this happen?' After all, it shouldn't have happened, according to the prevailing religious orthodoxy. God had promised his people a land, progeny and a special relationship, and the Exile made a nonsense of all three promises. This could have been, maybe even should have been, the end of that religious tradition of Yahweh altogether. This is a huge crisis for Yahweh. However, the D writers get God off the hook. They say, in effect, the reason this has happened is human sin and disobedience, represented in the failure to live up to covenant promises, and maintained most disastrously by a whole series of bad rulers. These books could be subtitled 'Decline and Fall'. For the D writers, the history of Israel is virtually a history of sin (thus connecting with one strain in the early chapters of Genesis); and the history of the monarchy is a history of failure and disaster. All of this is prefaced by the book of Deuteronomy itself, which stands as the theological statement that determines how the history is told. Some would even consider it a kind of constitution for Israel.

The whole thing is conveyed in a style reminiscent of tabloid journalism. There is an almost prurient enthusiasm for finding examples of just how bad things are, when human instinct is allowed free rein. Murder, dismemberment, gang rape of both men and women – it's a Sunday tabloid agenda.

Reflection on text

Read Judges 19.22–30. Do you think the author is writing this with a sense of sadness, or is he enjoying himself? How does the author achieve his aim of shocking his audience? Is it a shock to you to find such things written in the Bible? What adjustments does it mean one might have to make to the idea of the Bible as the inspired word of God?

That style is continued after the monarchy is established. This time it's just how corrupt are the celebs, and how their power has become a part of their downfall. The stories of king David's misdemeanours are told almost jauntily, and the descriptions of Solomon's greatness suggest more than a hint of irony as his wealth, his harem and his army appear to confirm the worst suspicions about the possible abuses a monarchy might bring. Then, as now, this style and theme connects with a religious strand which sees the conquest of personal sin as the main aim of religion. The writers present their audience with a choice in the face of crisis. The stark choice that is offered is life or death. There is no grey territory here. Such writing necessarily involves hyperbole. In the D writings that hyperbole is employed to emphasize not only how bad things are, and how corrupt are the celebs, and how stark is the choice; but also how great is the gift of God and how wonderful is the prospect of enjoying it. It is in this context that we should read the accounts of bloody battles in which God is ultimately responsible for mass slaughter and genocide. As we have seen, there is widespread scepticism about the historical accuracy of the accounts of Conquest and Settlement. But it is possible to get too hung up on all that and to miss the way in which the D theologians develop some themes that will be important for the future course of this religious tradition.

One of the key themes of D is that of **gift**. D writers emphasize that giving is one of the key attributes of God. This is a fundamental theological point. The alternative is to believe that humankind can win, deserve, or earn the good things that happen. The D view is that God has given and enabled them all. Indeed the people are specifically forbidden to boast of their conquest. 'You must not say to yourselves, "My own strength and energy have gained me this wealth." Remember the Lord your God; it is he who gives you strength to become prosperous' (Deuteronomy 8.17). Or again: 'Do not say to yourselves, "It is because of our merits that the Lord has brought us in to occupy this land . . ."' (9.4). Not only is the land seen as God's gift. The law is also a gift of God (as an alternative to chaos) (4.40). Also the Prophets themselves, the forerunners of the D writers, and to an extent their inspiration, are described as God's gift (18.15–20).

An extension of the idea that God gives, is that God chooses. The important theological idea of **election** derives from these writers (7.7–10). For the D writers this is always connected to the theme of the Covenant, which they develop. The phrase 'Ark of the Covenant', is a D invention (10.8). God's part in the agreement is to choose guide and save. His role will also ultimately be to judge. The appropriate human response is obedience, and a major section (chapters 12—25) of the book of Deuteronomy is devoted to detailed ordinances, fascinating in themselves, which deal with a huge variety of human circumstances: from the remission of debts every seven years (15.1–17), to the circumstances in which a man may be excused military service (20.5–9), and even to what happens to a woman who grabs a man by his genitals (25.11f.). All of this is placed in the context of the story of the Exodus. No opportunity is lost to recall that foundation story and its individual details. In particular it is placed in the context of the Sinai covenant and the ten words (commandments or commitments), which are rehearsed here with some interpretative addition (5.1–21).

What von Rad sees as the great credal assertion of Deuteronomy 6.4 that the Lord is one, probably bears witness in the first place more to henotheism than to **monotheism**. Henotheism is the belief that a god has absolute supremacy within geographical boundaries. We see this belief at 1 Samuel 26.20 and 2 Kings 5.17. Elsewhere there are still trials of strength for Yahweh to win, whether against Dagon (1 Samuel 5), or the prophets of Baal and Asherah (1 Kings 18). The message of D is that God is supreme in Israel, and the guarantor of this covenant community. However, the situation is not quite as simple as this. Bearing in mind that the D writings are finally edited at the time of the Exile, that is a context which is developing a more distinct monotheism. God is not just supreme in Israel but is the only God and will be the god of Israel wherever Israel is. The statements about God being one probably derive from a henotheistic tradition and background, but are expressed in a way that gives them monotheistic possibility. The one-ness of God is reflected in the D drive towards one nation and one sanctuary, or centre of religious excellence.

There is an ambivalence in these writings about whether or not the monarchy is a good thing. The pros and cons are spelt out in 1 Samuel 8 and 9. The message of chapter 8 is that monarchy will be a disaster and that the only 'king' the people need is Yahweh. The thrust of chapter 9 however is completely different. Here the view is that monarchy is a good idea in principle, but that it has been corrupted by bad kings. In effect, the readers are presented with a double whammy. Left to their own devices and without a king, anarchy reigns. But just when we thought it couldn't get any worse we are presented with kings who are themselves corrupt or useless. This is always presented in the context of a life-giving alternative. The readers of the D writings may be compared with those who read in John's Gospel that the light had come into the world but that people preferred darkness to light. And of course, remembering that this is an account with a post-Exile agenda, the whole thing is presented as warning and promise to a people who are wondering what they can now do to make their world safe and restore relations with God in a way that will give them access anew to his promises.

The message of the book of **Joshua** is that God enabled the conquest of the land of Canaan quickly and dramatically. As we have seen, this is more certainly a theological assertion than it is an historical one. The text itself points us to some of the issues.

- The land is large and populous but only a few set-piece battles are described, and they are described in terms of a standard formula (10.29–40).
- There are different versions of the way the land is given out in Joshua 13 as compared with Joshua 14—18.
- There are different versions of Joshua's calling the people together in chapters 23 and 24.
- There are clearly two traditions relating to the 12 stones placed in the Jordan evidenced at 4.8 and 4.20 as opposed to 4.9.
- There are clearly two different accounts of the battle of Ai (compare 8.3; 8.12).
- The king of Hebron is put to death twice (10.26; 10.37).

This kind of evidence prompts us to think that a number of sources might be involved, some of which are contradictory. But the real problem is between the theological assertion of a clean-sweep speedy conquest and whatever historical traditions the various sources bear witness to, which hint at a different story. We are told at 13.13 that the Israelites did not drive out the Geshurites or the Maacathites; at 15.63, that the Jebusites continued to live in Jerusalem; at 16.10, that the Canaanites who lived in Gezer continue to do so; at 17.11–13 that there is a whole string of towns which were not conquered; and at 17.16–18 that there are still Canaanites living in the country of Ephraim and Manasseh. This picture, together with other similar fragments, points us to a possible historical situation in which some refugees from Egypt gradually moved alongside people already living in the land. Their common socio-political interests rather than some ethnic identity, which were given purpose and focus by the stories these refugees told of a liberating God, Yahweh, are, it is more commonly claimed today, what led to the establishment of Israel. The climax of the book is the new recital of the 'history of Israel' together with a new commitment to the Covenant on behalf of all the people, this time made at Shechem (modern Nablus, hence its political sensitivity today, and its importance in Judaism) as described in Joshua 24 (especially vv. 26–8). It is interesting to compare this account with that in Exodus 24.

Reflection on text

Read the two accounts in Exodus 24.3–8 and Joshua 24.1–28 and notice the differences. In particular, consider which account dwells on the 'liberation' history; which dwells on the law, and which outlines the possible consequences of non-compliance. Do you think that the two groups of people concerned are 'signing-up' for the same reasons? If not, how would you describe the differences? Does this have any bearing on the reasons why people have a religious commitment today, do you think?

The book of **Judges** continues with the main theological theme of the power of God, the election of the people of Israel, and the gifts of God, as evidenced in the apportionment of land. Just as the gift of law itself provided a basis for social stability and security, so the gift of land is apportioned in ways that are fair and sustainable. The book has three main sections. 1.1—2.5 offers notes on the partial conquest; 2.6—16.31 describes the traditions of people called 'judges' who attempt to represent a unifying order in society in the absence of a king; and chapters 17—21 deal with issues unrelated to the judges as such but remind us of the main thrust of the author. With the advent of literary critical methods, the stories of people like Samson, Deborah and Gideon have attracted greater scrutiny, and there is generally less attempt to relate these accounts to historical backgrounds in the twelfth century BCE. But this is a relatively new study. The first narrative critical commentaries have only appeared since the mid-1990s. The D theology is most evident in the repeated refrain that there was no king in Israel, and that the people consistently did what was evil in the sight of the Lord. The principle is that success follows religious loyalty. Religious disloyalty, on the other hand, and disregard of the Covenant, leads to national weakness and foreign oppression. It is in this book that the tabloid style already noted is most in evidence.

The books of **Samuel** chart the movement from tribal confederation to kingdom. They focus on the rise of kingship as an institution. 1 Samuel is concerned primarily with Saul, Israel's first king. 2 Samuel is concerned with David, and the establishment of a new socio-political theological entity, 'The House of David', which is legitimized by the new form of covenant in 2 Samuel 7. This differs from its predecessor Sinai covenant, in that it is made with the establishment rather than with the people, and it appears unconditional. Both of these appear to have been seen by the D writers as part of the tragedy. They stress individual accountability and appear to be more on the side of the subversives than the establishment. This makes for some nice ironic writing where the authors appear to be praising their subject, but in fact are pointing to his weakness. Again it is perhaps worth pointing out that there is controversy over whether there is external evidence to support the accounts given. Although there is more written about David in the Bible than there is about Jesus, there is no other mention of him from ancient sources, and some writers (e.g. Whitelam) believe there was no such thing as a Davidic empire. From the D theological point of view it is important to 'talk up' this empire in order to emphasize the greatness of the gift, and by extension, the greatness of what has been lost through human disobedience. The so-called 'Court History' or 'Succession Narrative' begins in 2 Samuel 11. This describes the way in which David is finally succeeded by Solomon, as king. This is gripping and highly skilful narrative, which is far from innocent. Here we see in practice the dreadful cost which is paid for breaking the Covenant.

It is interesting that kings are judged not according to secular criteria but solely on religious criteria. In 2 Kings 18.1–8 we read a glowing account of the reign of King Hezekiah. 'He did what was right in the sight of the Lord . . . He trusted in the Lord the God of Israel . . . There was no-one like him in all the kings of Judah after him . . . He held fast to the Lord . . . He kept the commandments that the Lord commanded Moses.' He was king at the time that the king of Assyria besieged Judah, and that provides us with an alternative account of events that is nothing like as flattering to Hezekiah. By secular standards he made poor alliances and bought his way out of trouble with Assyria, but that is not how the account in 2 Kings tells it. Similarly, the story of Solomon's downfall is linked by the D writers exclusively to his toleration of foreign cults and shrines and his love of foreign women. This reign really signals the beginning of the end for a united Israel. In 722 Assyria conquered the northern province of Israel/Samaria, and thereafter the southern kingdom of Judah lives under an ever lengthening shadow until the Exile begins in 597, and that is where the books of **Kings** end, having given their coherent account of 'How could God let this happen? Why has this happened to us now? What lessons must we learn if we get a second chance?'

The newer literary critical techniques have moved scholarship away from questions about the relationship between what really happened and the biblical account. There is a new emphasis on the way the story is told, and in these books we have some of the best examples of storytelling in the Old Testament. Saul and David are both candidates for the title 'tragic hero'. David's flaws are all too obvious, and we see those which afflict Saul in, for example, 1 Samuel 28.5–20.

Reflection on text

Read 1 Samuel 27.1—28.20. This is a revealing account of two kings, David and Saul. After reading the account, do you think one is better fitted for kingship than the other? Are you satisfied by the arguments and justifications of the writer, or do you think the whole thing is unfair and arbitrary? How does this affect the way you read this as 'history'?

These become types of the flaws that undermine all Israel, and in the classic fashion of tragedy, flaws lead to downfall. Israel's story is then portrayed as a failure to live out their potential for greatness. These critical techniques have also given us permission to make connections with other parts of the tradition. So, for example, we can see a real connection between this practical account of Israel's behaviour, and the stories in Genesis 1—11. Both raise the same questions. Will God's will be frustrated by human corruption or will God's grace overcome human weakness? Will humankind opt for life or death? In these gripping and sometimes terrible narratives we see the issues as through the eyes of a religious tradition which is intense and uncompromising, but also (let's give them the benefit of the doubt) thrilling, inspiring and capable of application to our own day.

CHAPTER 8 SUMMARY

What is this chapter about?

This chapter is an introduction to the second of the main definitive theological strands in the Old Testament, namely that of the Priestly writings. There is some description of the contents of the books of Numbers and Leviticus, together with a more general discussion of the theological agenda and strategy of these writers.

What books are referred to?

The following new books are referred to: F. M. Cross, *Canaanite Myth and Hebrew Epic: Essays in the History and Religion of Israel* (Cambridge, Mass.: Harvard University Press, 1973), especially pp. 195–215; W. Brueggemann, *Cadences of Home* (Louisville: Westminster John Knox Press, 1997); Samuel E. Balentine, *Leviticus* (Louisville: Westminster John Knox Press, 2002); Norbert Lohfink, *Theology of the Pentateuch* (Edinburgh: T & T Clark, 1994).

What other books would be helpful?

The above list is probably sufficient on the specific topic, and contains bibliography which will point towards further study.

How is the chapter organized?

The chapter begins by looking at the relation between the D and P writings. There follows discussion about key themes in the writings, especially holiness, ritual and sacrament. This is followed by a rationale of the work as stemming from a perception of the absence of God.

What should I be able to do by the end of this chapter?

Distinguish the P writings.

Understand their historic context.

Provide exegesis based on the critical work done.

8

Wholeness and Holiness: The P Traditions

Alongside the D traditions of the Old Testament there is an alternative set of writings, which present their own response to the religious crisis of the Exile. These are the P traditions, deriving from a priestly background, and with a distinctive theology or set of theologies. It is usual today for scholars to see the juxtaposition of the two sets of traditions, D and P, in the Old Testament as the key to understanding the development in its religious thinking. This would be Brueggemannn's view, for example, as he believes that, 'The two interpretive traditions together constitute a formidable interpretive enterprise' (2003, p. 93). The inheritance of the P tradition is still evident in religious life today, and the juxtaposition is still part of what generates its dynamism.

Reflection on experience

As you read through this chapter, reflect on this assertion, and see what, if any, evidence you can find to support it. You might think of the importance of institutional religious life. You might also think of the growth of 'spirituality' as a main expression of the life of faith communities today, for example.

As we begin to consider these writings let us remember:

- That all the Old Testament writers have a reason for writing and an agenda which drives them;

- That the Old Testament does not present us with one unified view, but several, and that it is sometimes, as noted above, in the juxtaposition of these views (in so far as that allows a conversation between them) that truth emerges;
- That the so-called distinctive themes of the Old Testament actually come from a variety of sources, and are reworked by a variety of redactors; and
- That the crisis of the Exile must always be considered as a factor in later redactions.

We might also bear in mind two underlying 'themes' or issues, which have been suggested by our work so far. The first is the question of whether God's good intentions in creation will be inevitably subverted by corrupt humankind; or rather will God's grace inevitably overcome human frailty? The second is the tension between a God who guarantees order from chaos, and who speaks to kings, rulers and establishments to maintain law and stability, on the one hand; and, on the other, a God who is known as a liberator, who remembers and makes a covenant with a suffering people and who subverts and brings to nothing the thrones of the mighty.

The P writings are distributed throughout the Pentateuch more generally than the D writings. Most of the books of Leviticus and Numbers derive from this outlook, together with an alternative creation account, an alternative account or series of accounts about 'the fall', an alternative reflection on variety within creation, an alternative account of the setting up of the promises to Abraham, and an alternative vision of the implications of the Sinai experience. P is the latest of the contributors to the Pentateuch, and so, as its final redactor, is responsible for the final form. In fact some think that P's importance lies more in this redactional role, than as a source (so Cross 1973). It is important to note that there is nowadays much less tendency to ask the historical questions about the derivation of P, or to examine what it means to regard it as a unified source. It is, however, still thought useful to identify two main kinds of writing within the source, perhaps even two separate traditions. One contains the rules and ordinances for temple institutional life. The other is the P historical narrative or editorial tendency. These two sources or accounts have traditionally been identified as Ps and

Pg (the rather strange initials refer to German originals). The best recent attempted reconstruction of Pg is to be found in Lohfink (1994, p. 145, n. 29). Two other literary features are worth mention. One is the Holiness Code, Leviticus 17—26, sometimes referred to as H. The other is the recurring reference to 'the book of the generations of . . .'. Both of these may have been sources which predated P. The tendency now, though, is to concentrate on the content of P, rather than the historical process by which it came to a final form. Writers are more ready to identify P as a particular theological and religious strand, relating that to the situation which called for this new response (i.e. the Exile and its aftermath), and to other alternative theologies and responses (such as that of D). What connections, then, can we make between P and other Old Testament writings?

The connection between these writings and exile is subtly different from the connection between the D writings and exile. The D writers are attempting to answer the question, 'How could God let this happen?' They were doing their work at the beginning of the Exile when all seemed lost; and the theological insights gained there are the ones that drive the vision of the new Israel subsequently. The P writers are informed by later developments. They are responding to a more optimistic picture of a community emerging from exile, and attempting to answer the question, 'What do we need to do to survive with a religious identity in these new times: times when Israel will not be defined geographically, and which have to take account of new discoveries about God gained during exile?' In framing an answer they reflect on the things that have helped to maintain identity in exile conditions. Chief among them are: the institutions of religion, i.e. the ritual aspect of it all; male circumcision; and the keeping of the sabbath. All of these are marks of distinctiveness, which are hardly necessary until the people are stripped of the most basic mark of distinctiveness – a land. But having found them necessary, the P historical account embeds them in its tradition.

Reflection on text

To get a flavour of the P writings in the tradition from Genesis, read the following texts. Genesis 9.1–17 contains a universal promise of a restoration of peace and harmony; it also ties this to ordinances about boundaries with regard to food. In 17.1–27, the P version of the promise to Abraham, circumcision is made the central feature. In 28.1–9, boundaries are affirmed around whom it is possible to marry. And 46.6–27 is a typical genealogy, written in a stylized way to reach the conclusion that the symbolic number of seventy was involved.

Like the D writers, the P writers are associated with a new history of Israel. This time the history is told not to hunt for clues as to why bad things happened, but rather to search the story for clues as to how the community will continue in the future. This appears in our Bibles as 1 and 2 Chronicles, Ezra and Nehemiah.

There are connections between the P writers and the prophets, most noticeably with the later prophets of the Exile, Ezekiel and 2 Isaiah. Later prophets within the community that returned to Jerusalem after the Exile have much to say about the rebuilding of the temple, and that gives them a link of sorts with these priestly writings. The theme of holiness, introduced by 1 Isaiah in the eighth century, is one that the P writers develop.

Holiness is in fact a major theme of the writings, where it has a variety of layers of meaning. Perhaps the most common connects holiness with purity. God's good creation has been subverted by human agency: its purity has been defiled. Therefore it is an imperative of the religious life to get rid of all that defiles and return to the purity which God intended. The first half of **Leviticus**, in particular, deals with ritual ways of getting rid of defilement. These are probably among the least read bits of the Old Testament. The suspicion that many scholars, however objective they may claim to be, have in fact brought their religious baggage with them is never better demonstrated. Those who come from traditions that do not have involved ritual, or such clearly defined religious functionaries, tend to view Leviticus in a very negative light. Others, reading back from the bad press which priests and Levites usually receive in the New Testament Gospels, believe the post-exilic priestly system to have been at the heart of the decline and decay of Judaism, and they too have little sympathy with the P approach. It's a pity that the book's title is translated in this way. In Hebrew it is known by the opening words 'and he called', which though somewhat enigmatic, at least do not mislead.

One of the most important misconceptions about Leviticus in particular is that it is contributing to a view of priestliness that makes non-priests second class – a view very much at odds with much modern ecclesiology. In fact, although the first sixteen chapters are very much about rituals performed by priests, lay people are very much partners. In chapters 17–26, the Holiness Code is addressed to laity, so making the point that both priests and people need to attain to a kind of community holiness which will correspond to the hope of Exodus 19.6: 'You will be to me a kingdom of priests, a holy nation,' taken up in 1 Peter in the New Testament in a context which maintains that holiness is indivisible among the faithful.

These chapters are in fact a fascinating example of how theology is conveyed by transporting the reader to the point where they can imagine themselves part of a ritual, rather than inviting them to respond to a story. It's a bit like watching a play, particularly if there's lots of interaction between the players and the audience, rather than reading a novel. The basic theological idiom is twofold (so Balentine 2002, pp. 4f.). God has created the world to be harmonious, and wonderfully interconnected. God's creational order is mirrored by a ritual order, which in some way helps both to declare and sustain what God has done. This points us back to the P creation account in Genesis 1. This account is characterized by its liturgical movement to a harmonious climax. Boundaries and categories are important markers in this account. Each type of living thing is distinct. Each day has its own focus. But the result is an ordered and holy creation, which God approves. This account represents an invitation to worship (Balentine 2002, pp. 11–16), the very participation in which both declares and makes new. This is akin to what people nowadays would call a sacramental view of life and religion. According to this view the sacredness of all creation is honoured by those who are part of the called community, in a worship that declares God's deeds through symbol and drama, and which, it is claimed, helps a new state of affairs to come about. That is, worship is itself a part of the creative process.

Holiness is also used as a way of describing the relationship between people and God. The Holiness Code in Leviticus 17—26 contains the refrain 'I am the Lord your God', but in chapter 20 it is extended in this way: 'Hallow yourselves and be holy, because I am the Lord your God. Observe my statutes and obey them: I am the Lord who hallows you' (vv. 7f.). In other words the holiness of the people is based on the holiness of God. They are connected by holiness despite all the evidence of subversion and defilement. It was not a bad idea after all to create man in God's image. Humankind has holiness potential. Holiness is a theme that also connects with the gift of the land. The land itself can be defiled and needs to be purged. The whole thing is reminiscent of a campaign that was organized in the Coventry area around the time when the new cathedral there was about to be consecrated. The slogan was along the lines of, 'A consecrated people for a consecrated church' and it was making the point that holiness is not divisible. For those for whom holiness makes sense in terms of a world-view, there are implications in terms of behaviour, and indeed of community organization. And so the kinds of word that accompany and describe this world-view are words like holistic, gentle, healing, consecration, connectedness, harmonious, creative. They fit with a religious vocabulary of prayer, symbol, reflection, enactment and sacrament.

Reflection on text

Read Leviticus 18.24–30. Does the underlying conviction here about making sure the land is not defiled make any sense to you? This paragraph comes at the end of a section dealing with maintaining boundaries in human, and especially sexual, relationships. How does the underlying agenda of the writers affect your interpretation of these earlier sections?

Much of the debate about what a sacrament is, over the last five hundred years in the Christian community, have centred on questions about the presence of God. That too is an issue here. In fact, the real issue both in the P tradition and now, is the absence of God. We have seen how the JE tradition of the Pentateuch regarded God in an almost human way, as a good mate who can be spoken to directly. Later traditions emphasize God's distance and unpredictability to the point where, around the time of the Exile, the question of God's existence is an issue. The cry of the Psalmist 'How long?' well sums up the frustration of the faithful who want to see God do something. They want evidence. They want some sign, however tiny, that God is there, that he is somehow interested, and that at least some of the things they have believed about him in their cultural traditions are true. The P traditions contribute to this context of the perceived absence of God in three ways.

The first is to define God's holy space. This is the tabernacle, where God's presence can be dramatically realized. It is part of what for Balentine constitutes 'the boundaries and categories that enable a holy God to dwell in the midst of a world vulnerable to sin and defilement' (Balentine 2002, p. 4). It is possible, indeed probable, that many of the ritual occasions and ordinances for the sanctuary set out in Exodus and Leviticus were not a regular feature of life among the people of Israel at any stage (see for example Exodus 25—31; 35—40). In their way they are perhaps as idealized as the writings of the Deuteronomists. But the formalization of holy space does have the effect of making a statement of faith about God's presence, in much the same way that many church buildings do in today's world with all its evidence of God's absence. What it amounts to is that there are two ways of formulating faith and hope. One is the 'word' way, by telling stories to inspire and explain. The other is the 'sacrament' way, by enacting rituals which declare that faith and hope, and give some space to the faithful to explore what the world would look like if that faith were true and their hopes realized. Such enactment is a kind of 'as if' statement, very similar to that which can be seen in any Christian church, any Sunday. Everyone knows that that the world is full of hatred, and that destruction seems to have the upper hand; but in churches, people of faith and hope are acting out a ritual which suggests that for that time and space at least, forgiveness, sacrifice and love are a possible alternative which will in fact redeem the world. To read Leviticus and the other priestly writings from this perspective is perhaps to rescue them from the narrow obscurantism which all too often accompanies their discussion.

A second interesting suggestion as to how the P writings cope, from the perspective of faith, with the perceived absence of God, comes from Walter Brueggemann. He believes that among the experiences which exiled people had, was that of what he calls 'rootlessness' (Brueggemann 1997, p. 5). He believes that the genealogies, a particular feature of the P writings, are specifically designed to combat this by providing a sense of historical human connectedness. He is enthusiastic about the practical use to which these might be put. 'The recovery of these genealogies could indeed give an index of the mothers and fathers who have risked before us, who have hoped before us, and who continue even now to believe in us and hope for us' (1997, p. 5).

A third way in which we see the experience of God's absence contradicted, is through what seems like a throwaway phrase: 'God remembered' (e.g. Genesis 8.1; 9.15f.; 30.22; Exodus 2.24; 6.5; Leviticus 26.42).

Reflection on text

Read these references, from Genesis, Exodus and Leviticus. What is it in each case that God is remembering? How does this contribute to an understanding of the absence and presence of God, do you think?

The verb 'to remember' (*zakar*) is also used extensively in Deuteronomy, but here it is the people who are urged to remember the covenant they have signed up to. In the P tradition it is God who remembers. Just as the reason for using this word in Deuteronomy is because of the accusation that the people have forgotten; so the only reason to describe God's remembering in the P writings is surely to counter the popular perception that he has forgotten too.

So far we have used the word 'ritual' to describe the medium of the P writings, but a better term might be 'worship'. The liturgy of creation in Genesis 1 contains within it all that we shall find in the P traditions. As opposed to the JE tradition of creation, written in confident times, with man being created first and having sovereignty over the rest of creation, in the P tradition humankind is created last. And this is not so much as a climax to the whole drama, as it is suggesting that humankind comes lately to a creation which already possesses its own integrity and connectedness. Nevertheless the most comforting and affirming claim is made in this account that man is made in God's image. There is an inclusiveness in this account, not only in the way all 'orders of creation' are set out, but also in the way that humankind is created together: 'male and female he created them' (Genesis 1.28). The account is characterized by its formality: its liturgical feel and its insistence on boundaries and categories. In a remarkable way, the distance and awesomeness of God is held in balance with his accessibility. That accessibility is exemplified by God's speech, God's blessing, God's aesthetic approval and God's care for his creation; exemplified in his concern that humankind will have food to eat. This concern is to be mirrored in the stewardship humans are to display towards creation. (Some scholars believe that in Genesis 1.28 the words 'have dominion over' would be better translated 'have pastoral care for'.) The movement of the whole piece is towards harmony peace and rest as symbolized in the sabbath.

This is mature post-experience, post-trauma, religious writing, which complements, and to some extent stands in tension with, the writings of the D tradition. As the final redactors of the Pentateuch, the P writers have succeeded in writing a preface, which succinctly acts as an overture, containing the main themes and movements of what will follow. There is a sense among Old Testament scholars that the Pentateuch is 'canon' or 'scripture' in a more basic sense than any other part of the Old Testament. Just as the New Testament Epistles are in a sense derivative and stand as an interpretation of the message of the Gospels, so also it could be said that the rest of the Old Testament derives from the Pentateuch, the Law, the Torah.

CHAPTERS 9–12 SUMMARY

What are Chapters 9–12 about?

These four chapters may conveniently be regarded as a discrete section of
the book. They deal with prophecy and prophets. Chapter 9 is an introduction to the concept of prophecy, and Chapters 10 to 12 deal with the 'latter
prophets' section of the Hebrew Bible.

What books are referred to?

A. G. Auld, 'Prophecy and the prophets' in Stephen Bigger (ed.), *Creating
the Old Testament* (Oxford: Blackwell, 1989). (This book as a whole will be
of use in later chapters also.) T. H. Robinson, *Prophecy and the Prophets in
Ancient Israel* (London: Duckworth, 2nd edn 1953; R. E. Clements, *A Century
of Old Testament Study,* London: Lutterworth Press 1976; E Achtemeier,
Nahum–Malachi (Atlanta: John Knox Press, 1986).

What other books would be helpful?

In addition to the sections on prophecy in the general works already cited,
two readable introductions are: E. W. Heaton, *A Short Introduction to the
Old Testament Prophets,* 2nd edn (Oxford: Oneworld, 1996); John F. A.
Sawyer, *Prophecy and the Biblical Prophets,* 2nd edn (Oxford: Oxford University Press, 1993). There are too many commentaries to mention on the
books involved, and a browse through a good website or theological library
would identify what is likely to be most useful for specific books. The Abingdon and Interpretation series are reliable, mostly recent, and make an attempt to look at the applications of the texts.

How are the chapters organized?

Chapter 9 deals with the rise of prophecy. Chapter 10 with Amos, Hosea, Micah and the first part of Isaiah. Chapter 11 is concerned with Zephaniah, Nahum, Habakkuk, Jeremiah and Ezekiel. Chapter 12 looks at the remainder of Isaiah, Zechariah, Haggai, Joel and Obadiah.

What should I be able to do by the end of these chapters?

Describe the contents of the prophetic books.

Recount the major theological themes found in these books.

Relate these themes and their context to other writings in the Old Testament.

9

Introducing the Prophets

I well remember the kindly but rather innocent old buffer who first taught me about the Old Testament prophets. To the accompaniment of undergraduate sniggering, he told us that we were not to think of these people as men with crystal balls. We knew what he meant. In popular usage the term 'prophet' refers to those who can foretell the future. The role of Old Testament prophets was concerned more with their present and the way that would affect the future. So, for example, an Old Testament sort of prophet would not say, 'Next week you will go on a long journey and meet a tall, dark, handsome stranger,' but might well say, 'If you continue to smoke fifty cigarettes a day you will die prematurely.' But actually it's all rather less superficial than that. The key thing about prophets is that they introduce a new form of revelation from God. To people who believe that God's will and ways are conveyed by story, tradition and the rehearsal of these things in religious ceremonies, the prophets bring what is claimed to be the direct speech of God for a particular situation.

Reflection on experience

What does the term 'prophet' mean to you? Does it have some kind of predictive force, for example? Can you think of anyone whom you might consider a modern prophet? What is it about them that makes that title appropriate? How do you decide whether someone is a prophet or not? Is it important to know who is a true and who a false prophet? How might you distinguish between them?

The Old Testament canon distinguishes between the Former Prophets and the Latter Prophets. Between them these constitute the second element of the canon. The Former Prophets include the books we have described as the Deuteronomistic History from Joshua to 2 Kings. The Latter Prophets include the individual books of the named prophets Isaiah, Jeremiah and Ezekiel, together with a scroll containing twelve other prophetic works, variously known as The Book of the Twelve, or The Minor Prophets. The latter term is rather misleading because some of the books in this collection have contents which are far from minor in importance. Among the best known are Amos, Hosea, Micah and Habbakuk. Books about prophecy in the Old Testament have tended to concentrate on the Latter Prophets, and also tend to organize exegesis around the times in which the prophets lived. So successive chapters would deal with the prophets of the eighth century BCE, the prophets of the seventh century, and so on. For the prophets in this collection who offer some biographical details about their call as prophets, or about their former professions or family circumstances, there has been a temptation to relate exegesis very much to that biography. More recent scholarship is wary of this approach, considers much of the material in all the books to be composite, and is much more concerned to discern theological agendas, and establish connections with other parts of the tradition, especially the Torah.

A book like Isaiah presents a particular challenge. Traditionally it was studied according to the time-line scheme, acknowledging that different sections of the book date from different periods. So chapters 1—40 were studied in connection with the eighth century, chapters 40—55 were studied in relation to the exile years of the sixth century, and chapters 56—66 were studied as post-exilic. Now the tendency is to take the canonical end-product of the one book more seriously and to ask exegetical questions of the work as a whole, accepting also that the rather neat edges of the divisions set out above are not as neat as they seem. Nevertheless, in works which have as their distinguishing mark the immediacy of God's revelation, it is perhaps more helpful than otherwise to know something about the two important elements of any act of communication (apart from the message), namely the communicator and the context. The question is whether this information is in fact available to us from the text, and to this we shall return.

As far as the discerning of theological agendas is concerned, there is now more interest in making connections with the main theological agendas of the D and P writers. So, for example, the eighth- and seventh-century prophets are seen as having some relationship with the D writers, who may indeed have been responsible for collecting and maintaining their words and traditions. The prophet Ezekiel, on the other hand, together with some of the later prophets, is seen as having links with the P writings. The holiness traditions of Isaiah also find resonance with P, while some of the oracles from the middle (exilic) part of the book with their emphasis on judgement and forgiveness are more reminiscent of the D agenda. As these links are made, exegesis has become more 'suspicious'. After all, it is a very powerful thing to have the actual words of God ('thus says the Lord') to support one's position. This suspicion then leads to a larger degree of uncertainty about the usefulness of the prophetic books for sociological study, as if they were a record of fact. From the standpoint of sociological study, the prophetic writings make an important contribution to one of the questions we have identified as central to the Old Testament, namely, 'What is the relationship between religion and the state/establishment?' Is it the role of religion to uphold the order of the establishment, or is it rather the role of religion to interrogate the state, hold it accountable and offer alternatives that limit its sovereignty? Is religion propagandist or subversive – or indeed a mixture of the two? We shall see both tendencies as we study these writings more closely.

In so far as the Old Testament tells a story about the development of prophecy, it does so fairly unselfconsciously. It is possible to chart a development process through the Former Prophets, though this is far from easy, since several terms are used, apparently interchangeably, for the same kind of activity. The books certainly do not set out to provide an account of how prophecy develops, but it is interesting to look at the antecedents of the developed prophecy as exemplified in the Latter Prophets, as a way of helping to define what they were, and particularly what they were not. Whereas other ancient cultures had kings and priests, there is no exact equivalent in other cultures for the prophet as we read him described in a book like Isaiah. The Old Testament itself does make some reference to prophets from other religious groups (1 Kings 19.18). The two main ways of charting the beginnings of prophecy are (a) from the narrative accounts in the Former Prophets, and (b) from the polemic against false prophets, which is to be found in later writings.

The picture which emerges from a study of the narrative is of a society which is unsure how to access the answers to fundamental questions – the sort of questions where a declaration of some kind from God would be helpful. Superstitious means of accessing what is unseen and unknown are in evidence, such as drawing lots or consulting an oracle or medium. As nowadays, there often seems to be a fine line between what is received from such superstitious attempts, and genuinely religious revelation. Those who accurately foresee the future, or who are able to point to 'results' of some kind are granted a better hearing.

In this context, those who are described as prophets are usually anonymous. They appear to function in groups, perhaps with a leader, and are to be found either at a religious sanctuary or where the kings have easy access to them, which presumably means the royal court. At these places, they are supported, presumably, by the sanctuary or royal household. In other circumstances they act as paid consultants. People come to them with a problem, sometimes with money (e.g. Numbers 22.7), and they give a response. In order to do so they sometimes have to achieve a state of ecstasy, which is accomplished through music or possibly some kind of stimulant (see for example Isaiah 28.7), usually as a group activity. They are treated with a degree of suspicion, and described as odd or mad on occasion. This outline is then further coloured in by the polemic against false prophets to be found, for example, in Jeremiah 23.

Reflection on text

Read Jeremiah 23. From this invective, what would you say are the main features of a false prophet so far as Jeremiah is concerned? How does this help to define what a true prophet might look like?

As far as narrative accounts are concerned, a good place to start might be 1 Samuel 19.20–4. In this passage Saul is seeking David, to kill him. Successive bands of Saul's men are sent to Naioth to seize David, but each falls prey to the same fate. They see a group of prophets in a frenzy with Samuel at their head, and then they themselves fall into a frenzy. Eventually Saul himself goes to find David. He too then falls into a frenzy. (On his way to Naioth there is another interesting feature of the story. Saul enquires of an oracle as to David's whereabouts.) When Saul falls into a frenzy he also removes all his clothes. From this account we can see prophecy as a group activity, with a leader, associated with bizarre and frenzied behaviour. No word of God is connected to this phenomenon. If people want to find out the answers to questions or to seek the truth, they consult oracles. 2 Kings 9.11 gives another interesting insight into how prophets were perceived at this early stage. Elisha sends an unnamed prophet to tell Jehu: 'This is the word of the Lord the God of Israel: I anoint you king over Israel, the people of the Lord.' The prophet delivers his message to Jehu privately, drawing him aside from his companions. Having heard the message, Jehu rejoins them and they want to know what was said. They ask: 'What did that raving lunatic want?' And Jehu replies, 'Oh you know what he's like.' There is no vestige of respect here. Only the reader has respect, seeing that what the young man prophesied actually happens. But here, at least, there is a word from the Lord.

2 Kings 3.15–20 is an example of a prophet (Elisha in this case) being stimulated by music. Interestingly, one account of how David was introduced into Saul's court, in 1 Samuel 16.14–23, describes how Saul needs music to ward off an evil spirit. Music was obviously seen not just as something soothing and pleasant, but rather as giving access to a spirit world. Saul is associated with several means of trying to access hidden truth. 1 Samuel 14.41f. sees him engaged in a 'heads or tails' kind of lot-drawing ceremony (urim and thummim). 1 Samuel 28.3ff. again sees Saul in a quandary. God does not speak to him through dreams, nor by casting lots nor by the prophets. And so he consults a medium, and by that means does actually get to speak with the dead Samuel. This is regarded as beyond the bounds of what is permissible, and a crucial event in his downfall.

But, these hints apart, from a theological point of view, the most interesting thing about these group consultant-style prophets is that they stand accused of telling their paymasters what they want to hear. That is, they are false prophets. They preach a false optimism. Jeremiah 23 sets out their shortcomings in detail and identifies the key difference between such false, and true prophets: 'If they had stood in my council, they would have proclaimed my words to my people' (Jeremiah 23.22). True prophets are those who have in fact stood in the very council of YHWH, and been prepared to say things which are unpopular and against the grain of popular opinion and sentiment. In the narrative, we can see the distinction beginning to develop, in the series of stories about Elijah and his contemporaries in 1 Kings 18—22.

- 1 Kings 18.22 sees Elijah setting out the significance of God's revelation. This is not something so superficial or indulgent as a horoscope: this is about which God you follow, and a decision must be made. 1 Kings 19 shows that Elijah does 'stand in the council of YHWH'. YHWH confides in him what the future will be, and despite Elijah's feeling that he alone is left of the faithful, he is commissioned to deliver the messages to inaugurate the future as described.

- In 1 Kings 21 we read the story of Naboth's vineyard, which describes an appalling human rights violation by King Ahab, in concert with his wife Jezebel, as they kill a small farmer in order to gain his land. Being the king, he might expect to get away with it, but no longer. Elijah acts in the prophetic role of defending a higher morality than that of the state. Kings are themselves accountable to God. They do not determine what is right and wrong. Elijah goes to see Ahab and pronounce God's judgement on him. (We might be reminded here of Nathan's visit to David after his adultery with Bathsheba, in 2 Samuel 12.)

- Then in 1 Kings 22 we have the story of Micaiah. The kings of Israel and Judah want to wage war to recover the enclave of Ramoth-Gilead, but feel the need to consult God first to make sure victory will be theirs. All the court prophets prophesied victory. One of them, Zedekiah, went so far as to perform the dramatic act of making iron horns and asserting that the kings would gore their adversary (the king of Aram) just as one might be gored by these horns. Heavy stuff. Micaiah is consulted last of all, and reluctantly, because his prophecy, it seems, is usually counter-cultural. This is so once again as he prophesies defeat for the two kings. Micaiah is laughed to scorn and imprisoned, but his prophecy proves to be correct.

Reflection on text

Read 1 Kings 22.1–38. How effectively do you think the author demonstrates the difference between true and false prophets in this passage? Do prophets have to be unpopular to be truthful, do you think?

As we see the emergence of this new breed of prophet we are better able to define the characteristics of the later prophets. They are independent of guilds or gangs: unrelated to courts or sanctuaries. They require no stimulus, assume no frenzy, work no miracles, and take no reward. They are not consultants, responding to requests. They speak the word of the Lord as it is given to them. Being a prophet is not a carefully considered career option for them. Becoming a prophet has been their vocation, something they cannot resist, and something that is against all the odds. The biographical details appear at pains to bear this out (e.g. Amos 7.14). There have been suggestions that the term 'prophet' which is disavowed by Amos and others was really a term of something like abuse in their own day, and that it only came to occupy the place it now has in the tradition as a result of post-exilic editorial hindsight. '[These Latter Prophets] . . . would not have been seen dead as prophets!' (Auld 1989, p. 204). Narrative plays a relatively minor part in the latter pre-exilic prophets. The oracles – what God says through the prophets – are all-important. And that word is often counter-cultural and unpopular. From the standpoint of the writers and biblical editors, the key thing is that the people and their rulers were wrong and God was right. This is the D message by other means. The extent to which it relates to historical reality is something we shall return to as we look at the prophets of the eighth century.

Certainly, though, the term 'prophets' comes to relate more and more to a body of writings and less to historic figures. Interesting questions can be asked about why, if these prophecies were so time-specific and place-specific they should have been collected, saved and handed on at all. The probable answers are (a) the oracles could be used as part of the apologetic of specific theological groups such as the D writers; and (b) some thought that this revelation was of such universal significance that it could be re-applied to other situations. On the one hand, we have re-application theses, which refer to the Old Testament community itself. So Brueggemann can assert, 'the prophetic canon functions as a resource to protect the community of faith from surrendering to the vagaries of historical circumstance' (2003, p. 108). On the other hand we have the kind of messianic interpretation of the prophets started by the early Christians and maintained ever since by the more conservative interpreters. According to this reading, the prophets' message was only partly directed towards the situation in their own time. It was also partly, or indeed mainly, directed towards the birth, ministry and death of Jesus. Such interpretation can be seen as early as the Gospel of Matthew, who wants to demonstrate that Jesus is in fact the one sent by God and expected by the people. We do need to recall, perhaps, that much early Christian apologetic took the form of seeing Jesus as the realization of Old Testament prophecy. Less conservative interpretation has tended to emphasize the message of the prophets for their own generation, and to stress the theme of justice, though as liberation theologians point out, a great deal of work needs to be done to discern what the implications of that justice are.

In general introductions to the prophetic books, some commentators attempt to write a chapter on 'the message of the prophets' or equivalent titles. We should remember that as recently as the end of the nineteenth century, scholars still believed that the 'message of the prophets' was the heart of the Old Testament, for Christians especially. It was seen as exploring the implications of **ethical monotheism**. Little changed in the way 'the message of the prophets' was interpreted for almost the whole of the next century. Theodore H. Robinson, writing in the preface to the second edition of his *Prophecy and the Prophets in Ancient Israel*, in 1953, can say that in most respects little had changed since the first edition of 1923. In R. E. Clements' *A Century of Old Testament Study* (1976) the greater part of the discussion revolves around the scholars of the turn of the century. Themes which are consistent enough to be included in more modern summaries include: salvation, righteousness, Zion, the Day of the Lord and social justice. But the usefulness of such lists is questionable. If more recent commentators are correct in linking the prophets to particular schools of theological thought, and linking that in turn to their relation to the Exile, then a theme like 'salvation' will actually have several different readings and possible meanings throughout the corpus. A theme like 'The Day of the Lord' needs to be related to the whole eschatological longing and expectation of Israel. This is evidenced in different ways by different theological schools, and again in relation to the Exile. Other commentators discuss whether judgement or hope are dominant motifs in particular books. When seen in relation to the agendas of D and P we might expect that the theme of judgement would be uppermost in the D-oriented pre-exilic and exilic writings; and that hope would be a dominant theme thereafter, and that is largely what we find. Some want to see an intentional editing process arranged around the themes of judgement and restoration, or judgement and hope (see Brueggemann 2003, p. 107).

The books of the Latter Prophets are not verbatim accounts of what the named prophets said. That being said, they probably do contain remembered words of honoured figures, but their organization is often chaotic, and oracles from other sources and, perhaps, original editorial material are mixed in a way which it is difficult and probably fruitless to disentangle. The key characteristic of this part of the canon remains that it introduces a new and immediate, and therefore powerful, source of God's revelation, and that it does so in relation to a political and social world that is still recognizable to us. Importantly also, these writings critique the community of faith, its functionaries and its ceremonies. They become the immediate source of religious energy for some creative generations of theologians. They become the raw material from which the hopes and faith of the people of YHWH will be fashioned, and which will eventually shape the content and dynamics of Christianity. In comparison with the mid-years of the last century this conclusion and assessment may seem quite radical. If I had a crystal ball I would say that in retrospect it will not have been half radical enough.

10

Even the Good Times are Bad

I remember growing up during the 1960s in Britain. They were wonderful revolutionary times. We felt that humankind had come of age: that the aggression and austerity that had characterized our parents, influenced by wartime experience, had given way to a new gentleness and inclusiveness. It was a time of innovation, of freedom and of new possibility as a whole generation opted vociferously for peace and love. However, forty years on, and we hear the British Prime Minister saying that actually the 1960s are at the root of all our modern ills in society. Some are happy to believe that (especially if they weren't there and have nothing invested in those times), while others are suspicious about his motives. Does he want to blame the Sixties to draw attention away from other possible causes in which his political party may be implicated? For whom does he speak? Not, certainly, for the many in my generation who appear to feel that important things have been lost to society, and that actually they were the times we need to learn from, but in an applied way.

Reflection on experience

Have you ever had the experience of hearing someone 'rewrite' history in this way? War veterans, for example, are often horrified to hear, years later, that what were regarded at the time as acts of heroism, are later thought of as acts of unnecessary barbarism. George Orwell's book, *1984*, describes a Government Department whose sole purpose is to rewrite history. To what extent do you think this is a legitimate part of civilized development?

Social commentary is a very precarious thing whose interpretation, even when it refers to the recent past, is far from simple, and it is good to refer to our own experience in this matter when we read the books which form the Latter Prophets section of the Old Testament. It is easy to read these books as if:

- They express a majority view, or one that would at least appear clear and sensible to all right thinking people;
- They provide accurate historical data, which can help us to reconstruct accurately, social conditions at specific times and in specific places;
- They contain the verbatim words of the prophets named in the titles, without editorial development; and so
- They are theologically innocent.

We need to remember that none of these is necessarily true.

There is a convention that the prophets are studied using the critical methods appropriate for history. That means that the first chapter in most books about the Latter Prophets will begin with the prophets of the eighth century BCE. We shall stick to this convention and look at these prophets presently, but it is worth noting that new attempts are now being made to study the prophets 'canonically'; that is, to see them in relation to their received literary context rather than their supposed historical one. This study is most advanced in relation, first, to Isaiah, which as noted is no longer studied as if it were three books tagged together, but rather with the assumption that there may be a final editorial hand at work in the whole document. The Minor Prophets, or Book of the Twelve is also offering fruitful new pastures for literary critics who want to know if there is significance in the way the books are ordered in the collection.

To study the texts historically is to read them against a background of events (sometimes, it must be said, pieced together only from biblical sources), of which the most important points are as follows.

Following the death of Solomon, his son Rehoboam, showing, according to 1 Kings 12, a remarkable degree of political ineptitude, managed to alienate the people of the north – the area called Israel. From around 930, the two areas that had formed a united kingdom under David and Solomon, that is,

Israel in the north and Judah in the south, became two separate kingdoms. The capital of Judah was Jerusalem, and the capital of Israel was first Tirzah, and then subsequently, Samaria, a new and somewhat glamorous city. They were never again to be united, and over time, as the New Testament bears witness, they became bitter enemies. We hear far more in the Old Testament from the southern perspective of Judah than from the northern one of Israel. On the face of it, Israel looks like the more interesting place to live. The northern country is more fertile, has access to the sea and, being more open to trade from the northern areas which make up modern Lebanon, is the more cosmopolitan. The first king, Jeroboam, tried to maintain the folk-memory of YHWH religion, but with an individual northern twist which has the effect of making Jerusalem less important. However, his rather innovative plan did not work, and the impression given to us the readers is that YHWH was unhappy with the north. In addition, its cosmopolitan setting meant that it had more contact with non-YHWH religions. Successive kings did not opt for an exclusivist YHWH enclave in Israel. They were happy to see something more pluralistic develop. This too was held against them. The rationale we are presented with in the books of our Old Testament is, that since they were not true successors of David, then what could you expect?

As we read the history, this religious behaviour is held responsible for everything that went wrong subsequently. Many kings of the north were assassinated and the history was bloody. Notoriously bad kings, like Ahab, whose wife was Jezebel, were of the north. Israel had two powerful neighbours to the north-east, Damascus and Assyria. Israel formed alliances with or fought wars against Damascus throughout the ninth century. But there was a period during the eighth century when Damascus was fighting a prolonged war against Assyria (which it ultimately lost), when Israel enjoyed a deal of peace and prosperity. In the north, this came to an end in 722 when, having conquered the 'buffer zone' of Damascus. Assyria conquered Samaria. Many of its inhabitants were deported, but there were also new settlers with their own religious traditions. This meant that Samaria became pluralistic in every sense. Its inhabitants were not pure-bred Israelites and a kind of YHWH religion coexisted with other expressions of religion. We hear few voices from this community, which experienced disaster and exile 140 years before the south. The E traditions of the Pentateuch give us one supposed northern source. Elements of the book of Deuteronomy also have their origins in the north. With so little material from the north, two prophets of the eighth century, from the north, have therefore been regarded as key witnesses to the religious consciousness there. They are Hosea and Amos.

In the south, the kingdom of Judah was not unaffected by these international developments. Its economy was based more on pastoral farming, and it looked towards Egypt and Arabia as trading partners. It too enjoyed a period of peace and security in the eighth century as the northern kingdoms were slugging it out. But as 2 Kings 16 records, when it came to the crunch for the three small kingdoms, the king of Judah, Ahaz, refused to join with Israel and Damascus against Assyria; preferring rather to appeal to Assyria for help against Israel. This action was regarded as contributory to the downfall of Israel, and the account in 2 Kings is not complimentary. However, Ahaz's son Hezekiah gets a good press in the D history ('He did what was right in the eyes of the Lord, as his ancestor David had done', 2 Kings 18.3). He it was who resisted the advance of the Assyrian king Sennacherib against Jerusalem in 701, despite being put under siege for a considerable time. Eventually the siege was lifted. Hezekiah had to buy his way out of trouble, and it may be that some epidemic among the Assyrians influenced events (2 Kings 19.35). But at least the day was saved. The initial prophecies of Isaiah date from this very anxious period, as do those of Micah. The arrangement of the prophetic books and their juxtaposition in the canon may owe something to an attempt to compare the fate of Judah and Israel respectively, according to theological principles.

Whether or not this account of history is factually reliable, it *is* the background against which we are meant to read and interpret the prophecies of the period. What we are asked to see, in both north and south, is how even when times seem good and prosperous, if the demands of God are neglected, disaster will follow. The prophets of this period are portrayed as declaring, with degrees of unwillingness, a message which recalls the people, their rulers, and the movers and shakers in society generally, to their special status and special responsibility, particularly in relation to the Covenant. This is a time of theological creativity, and it is interesting that it is generated in a society with which many people would have been very satisfied. It is during this period that the J (south) and E (north) histories are being put together, and the beginnings of the covenant theology that will so dominate the writings of the D school and especially the book of Deuteronomy itself, is beginning to take shape. Each of the four prophetic books of the period has its own particular character, and collectively they are among the most memorable writings in the Old Testament.

Reflection on text

Read Amos 2.4–12. Here we see typical Amos themes. The Covenant has been broken. The scandals are most evident in the lack of respect for the poor, and in the way that religious observance has been subverted. Note both the content and the style. Is this a text that has easy application to your own situation?

The book of **Amos** is a good place to start. We are given a picture here of how religion can be corrupted in times of prosperity. This shows a people unaware of the links between morality and religion, or between culture and religion or in fact between public life and religion. Religion has been relegated to a ceremonial role, largely outmoded, in which the meaning of rituals and observances has long since been forgotten, with little more than nuisance value to those who want to get on with the real business of life, namely making money (8.4–7). This society is not sustainable, and much of the book of Amos is concerned with indictment against its excess, injustice and essential godlessness. The book has three main sections. Chapters 1 and 2 are oracles against the nations. This is a familiar prophetic literary device to demonstrate YHWH's sovereignty over all nations and not just Israel. YHWH has a public role. It is interesting that these oracles include allegations against both Israel and Judah. The reference to Judah (2.4f.) is probably a later addition, providing evidence that the book was probably used and revised in a new situation in Judah after its initial reference to Israel. Chapters 3—6 are typical prophetic oracles outlining Israel's wrongdoing and the punishment that will follow. It includes the introduction of the term 'The Day of the Lord' (5.18), to which we shall return. That heightens, in the third section, chapters 7—9 in which a series of visions outlines coming judgement, and in particular the deportation to Assyria. This is seen not as some unconnected political act, but as the judgement of God. A final section 9.11–15 appears to be a later addition which is completely at odds with the rest of the book, providing a message of hope and restoration: further evidence of later creative editorial work based on theological reflection in a different context. However we read this kind of work, we need to have a strategy which sees this kind of continuing editorial activity as completely legitimate.

The truth of the matter is that the prophet's words have been seen as vital and appropriate in all sorts of situations during the past two and a half thousand years. It is little wonder that they have been moulded in use. Among the memorable charges are those of injustice and corruption. 'They sell honest folk for silver, and the poor for a pair of sandals. They grind the heads of the helpless into the dust, and push the humble out of their way' (2.6f.); '. . . what do they care for straight dealing who hoard in their palaces the gains of violence and plundering?' (3.10); '. . . you Bashan cows on the hill of Samaria who oppress the helpless and grind down the poor . . .' (4.1); 'you levy taxes on the poor and extort a tribute of grain from them' (5.11). Judgement will follow. 'Woe betide those living at ease in Zion, and those complacent on the hill of Samaria' (6.1). If you lived in Zion (i.e. Jerusalem) and had read thus far, you would be aware of what had already happened in Samaria, and these words would no doubt have had real force. The charge against the parody of religion is no less fierce. 'I spurn with loathing your pilgrim feasts; I take no pleasure in your sacred ceremonies' (5.21). Religion has itself become part of the problem. 'Father and son resort to the temple girls, so profaning my holy name. Men lie down beside every altar on garments held in pledge, and in the house of their God they drink wine on the proceeds of fines' (2.7f.).

The antidote to this is to rescue the link between religion and morality and pursue the case for religion as something of public significance. Justice and righteousness are the key characteristics of a society in which these connections are properly made, and the significance honoured (5.15, 24). The language of relationship and covenant is employed to supply the rationale. Judgement is coming because YHWH developed a special relationship with this people, and he has been betrayed (2.9–11; 3.2; 5.14, 24; 8.2). What is now required is a new culture which accords sovereignty to YHWH and so acknowledges and responds to his gifts; a culture which picks up themes of responsibility and accountability, and a religion which is based on a covenant echoing the Sinai themes of justice, righteousness, truth and a relationship with a living and involved God.

Reflection on text

Read Hosea 3. Note the difference in style and tone between this and Amos. This is part of the biography of Hosea, in which his relationships are taken as a model of that between God and Israel. How appropriate a model do you think it is, in describing the relationship, between God and humankind, to compare this union to that of a man with his unfaithful wife?

The canon itself begins with **Hosea**, the first book in the Book of the Twelve, the other representative of the north. This book, too, takes the necessity of faithfulness to YHWH in covenant, as its basic theme. But the most striking thing about the book is that the message is portrayed against the dramatic background of a broken and flawed marriage. While there is some dispute about exactly how much of the material is truly autobiographical, there is no doubt about the passion and force of the writing, nor that it is meant to be read as autobiographical. It is usual to examine the book in two sections. Chapters 1—3 deal with the marriage, breakdown and renewal of Hosea and his wife Gomer. Chapters 4—14 include a series of accusations against Israel, sometimes reworked to have reference to Judah, set out as lawsuits. The tender language and ethos of the first three chapters is reflected in the second section when YHWH is being described. 11.1–9 begins, 'When Israel was a youth, I loved him,' and continues with such sentiments as: 'It was I who taught Ephraim to walk, I who took them in my arms . . . I led them with bonds of love . . . I lifted them like a little child to my cheek' (11.3f.). The climax of the passage describes how these bonds of love are stronger than Israel's sin, 'A change of heart moves me, tenderness kindles within me' (11.8). It is impossible for God to let the relationship go. And the reason is that he is God and not mortal (11.9).

The first three chapters introduce the prophet's revelation about the nature of YHWH as he reflects on his marital history, and reflects on how that mirrors the relationship of God with Israel. Hosea marries a prostitute who bears him children (all with symbolic names that are suggestive to the people of Israel, such as 'not my people' or 'not loved any more'). Gomer then continues her life of prostitution and Hosea is angry. Though she fancies that it might be better for her to return to him (2.7), his thoughts are of revenge and retribution. Then, against all the odds of what, until now, has been a story with which many could identify, there is an intervention which is nothing short of miraculous. 'But now I shall woo her, lead her into the wilderness, and speak words of encouragement to her' (2.14). That is, despite everything he has her back, and not grudgingly but delightedly.

The book has a number of features in common with other prophet books.

- The work as we have it is obviously the result of a long process of editorial reworking, as a consequence of applying the basic message to new situations. This kind of reflection is the way theology is done and is both legitimate and desirable. It shows the vitality of the community of faith. A message once designed for eighth-century Israel can be reapplied to seventh-century Judah, and used by post-exilic communities in both north and south as a means of interpreting God's will for them.
- The book's message, although heavy with judgement, is not simply a prophecy of doom. This is a message of both judgement and hope. It is, in effect, about exile and restoration.
- The book tells us something immediate about the nature of God. This has been a new sighting, a new insight.

Its characteristic message to society, though, is that for society to be sustainable, it must have a culture of relationship at its heart. That is, members of society must feel a sense of connectedness with each other, and as if each has a stake in the other's destiny. Relationship terms like love, healing, forgiveness and grace are not restricted to the private domain. They are words that have public significance. Some years ago I remember a church movement which argued that there must be forgiveness in politics. The group was formed in relation to the problems between Britain and Ireland at the time, but there is an ongoing issue here, which has resonance in places like the Balkan states and the Middle East. Does something as personal and intimate as forgiveness have a role in the public domain of politics and peacemaking? Hosea's answer would be, yes.

Traditionally we should include **Isaiah** 1—39 in this eighth-century survey. Accepting the information from the book itself, this contains the prophecies of Isaiah of Jerusalem who was a member of the upper social classes, with an understanding of the role of priests (assumed from the temple vision of chapter 6), and king (7.3; 8.2) in the mid-years of the eighth century. More recent textual study has arrived at a more complicated consensus. Chapters 1—12 are seen as the most important eighth-century materials. These relate to the anxious times already outlined when King Ahaz (or Uzziah) ruled. Hezekiah's reign is thought to be reflected in the prophecies of chapters 28—33, and 36—39. This last should be read in conjunction with 2 Kings 18—20. These sections also reflect the themes of judgement and promise: disaster and renewal. The city of Jerusalem comes to have more importance here as you would expect. The passages that represent later additions to the early material are responses to that perspective, that YHWH is committed to Jerusalem. They would include chapters 13—23, a series of oracles against the nations, demonstrating YHWH's sovereignty, and heightening the sense of privilege which Jerusalem enjoys. Chapters 34 and 35 quite clearly speak of a post-exilic return to Jerusalem, and belong more properly with the late exilic oracles to be found later in the book. Chapters 24—27, the so-called Isaiah apocalypse, we shall consider separately, later. For now, the main feature to note is the way in which the Zion/Jerusalem tradition is developed not only to be a symbol of hope for returning exiles, but rather a cipher for the hopes of the whole world. The destiny of the world, and the final resolution of its problems, will be focused here.

Reflection on text

Read Isaiah 11.1–10. What are the chief characteristics of this ideal future? Note the importance of David, and so Jerusalem. Note also the key areas of peace, harmony with nature, and social justice.

Just as with the prophets of the north, we saw the possibility of an intentional linkage between the 722 Deportation and the 587 Exile from Judah, so in the final form of these chapters we may see a linkage between 722 and 701. That is, whereas Israel fell to Assyria in 722/1, Judah held out against Assyria in the siege of Sennacherib. This is the gift of YHWH and a sign of his commitment to Jerusalem. By extension there may be an intentional linkage between 701 and 587, and the crisis management of those times respectively. The first new theological theme which Isaiah introduces, and which runs through the whole book, is the greatness of God. In the vision in chapter 6 this is seen in terms of his holy awesomeness. As the book develops we come to see a God who is sovereign over nations, over creation and over history. In such a God there can be confidence. The second theme, already noted, is the importance of Jerusalem in the tradition. Allied to this are the seeds of a messianic expectation which will continue to flourish and flower, and which provides categories of interpretation for the New Testament church as they seek to understand the significance of Jesus.

The prophet **Micah** was probably a contemporary of Isaiah. The book is typical of what we have seen of eighth-century prophets. It contains some original material (chapters 1—3 and 6) with some reworking and new theology, so that the finished product reflects the judgement and hope, punishment and restoration theme. Of special interest is the perspective of an author who comes not from the royal courts and corridors of power, but from the countryside, where the effects of economic exploitation are particularly acute. 'Woe betide those who lie in bed planning evil and wicked deeds, and rise at daybreak to do them, knowing that they have the power to do evil! They covet fields and take them by force; if they want a house they seize it' 2.1f.). These prophecies are not about international politics but social justice. The later oracles about restoration echo the themes of the prophets we have seen, sometimes closely (cf. Micah 4.1–5; Isaiah 2.2–6), though perhaps with a rural perspective. Of particular interest is 6.6–8, which some regard as a summary of the message of the eighth-century prophetic message in total. That is a message about the covenant relationship; about a society that needs to consider its destiny and purpose more fundamentally, and about a religious establishment which has become totally marginalized. The difference between the prophets and their audiences, one suspects, is that the audiences considered that the good days would go on for ever, whereas the prophets perversely saw that the good times were unsustainable and that the inevitable collapse would only be rescued and new society possible by the grace and gift of God.

11

A Time for Reflection

It is common to group most of the prophets we shall look at in this chapter as 'seventh-century', just as those of the last chapter were 'eighth-century', but that can give the impression of an easy progression or development of prophecy, and that impression would be quite wrong. After the prophecies of Isaiah and Micah in Judah, no new prophetic voice is available to us for about another seventy years, and then several arrive together. How was religious life sustained then, in the intervening years? What resources were available to access the direct word of God? As we have seen, the words of the northern prophets, Hosea and Amos, were handed on, revised and edited for local use in Judah, prior to the crises of 701. But these were words for crisis, and the next looming crisis did not appear until very late in the seventh century. It is generally assumed that the E traditions of the Pentateuch were brought to the south by refugees and combined with the J source sometime during this period. The core of the D tradition, which was to come to full flower later in the century, also came from the north. The words of the southern eighth-century prophets were available. This then was the material on which the faithful could reflect as they tried to answer the questions their experience had raised for them.

And those questions, read against the assumed historical background that the editors intend, are raised by three political issues that have religious implications.

- The first is the fall of Samaria, the northern kingdom, in 722/1.
- The second is the siege of Jerusalem and the consequent failure of Assyria to take the city, in 701.
- The third is not a specific event but the unfolding of imperial history in the area during the seventh century BCE.

What are the religious implications? The first of these events, the fall of Samaria, was a precursor of the Exile to Babylon, which was apparently such a seminal event in the subsequent history of the Old Testament. It raised the same kinds of religious question. Those in the north considered themselves to be heirs to all the same promises that had been made to those in the south. God had promised them land, progeny and a special relationship. They might also have assumed that alongside these promises was a guarantee of peace, of 'shalom', of the ability to enjoy that which God had provided. What had actually happened was that apart from a relatively brief period of around seventy years, their territory had been fought over in the bloodiest possible way, and the final outcome had been the end of their possession of the land as they were deported to Assyria. In fact in many ways it was worse, from a religious point of view, than the Exile to Babylon, because in the case of the north, the land was settled, in their stead, by strangers and foreigners. In such circumstances as these what chance was there of maintaining progeny: descendants who were true Israelites? What possible evidence could there be for a special relationship?

Hardly less puzzling was the 'success' of Hezekiah in resisting the Assyrian advance of Sennacherib in 701. How was this to be read? From one perspective it was indeed a humiliation for Judah, and the price that had to be paid weakened the country fatally. But at least the land was maintained and the religion of YHWH had a home. The political events of the new seventh century (i.e. the 600s) were not easy to read from a religious point of view. What was God doing here and why? In the early part of the century the kings of Judah were in effect vassals of Assyria, the main imperial power in the area. Around the middle of the century Assyria's power began to be challenged by the emerging influence of the Medes, coming from present-day Iran; the Chaldeans, coming from Iraq; and the Egyptians. The result of their rise to power was the defeat of Assyria. Nineveh, the Assyrian capital, fell in 612, and that was the end of them. The victors then had a period of sorting out the region between and among themselves, which resulted in Babylon being the main political force in the area, challenged by Egypt. Politically, the rulers of Judah, strategically placed between Babylon and Egypt, had to decide whether it was in their interests to form an alliance with one against the other. These were very uncertain times in which the extreme vulnerability of Judah was placed in sharp focus. And so, from a religious perspective, if Judah were to escape the fate of Samaria, what lessons were to be learned? Why had God allowed Samaria to fall? What message was he trying to send them in arranging the politics of the region thus? Was there anything that could be done? What religious issues should dominate decision-making? Would the God who had spared Judah once under Hezekiah spare her again?

Reflection on experience

We are now in a better position to see how reflecting theologically on events is one of the main activities of the Old Testament writers. They were not so much concerned with philosophical questions about God's existence, or with systematic theological speculation on themes such as sin and judgement. Rather they asked questions like: 'Where is God in all this?' 'How do we discern what he is trying to say to us?' 'What is our best course?' Which of these approaches to the business of theology attracts you most? Does your answer have any effect on how you read the Bible?

It was against this background that King Josiah came to the throne in 640. He would reign until 609 when he would be killed at the Megiddo gap, getting caught between Egypt and Babylon. (Megiddo has huge strategic importance as a route centre. Consequently some of the most important wars in the area were fought there. That is why, in extreme visions of massacre and disaster, the area is used as a pictorial example, as Armageddon.) Josiah is portrayed as a reforming king (an account of his reign is to be found in 2 Kings 22, 23). The D historians regard him as their main hope of restoring the religion of YHWH. As we have seen, he was responsible for a programme of reform which included limiting public religious life to a centre of excellence in Jerusalem, and instigating a new context for the observance and transmission of religion: the home. You can almost imagine him describing his programme as 'education, education, education'. Since we only know about these reforms from those who in any case supported them, it is difficult to assess their impact or indeed to know whether what is described is aspiration or fact. Writings which emerge in something like a canonical form from this period of reflection include: the Deuteronomic writings, the beginnings of the books of the eighth-century prophets, and the pre-exilic Pentateuchal material. The D answer to the questions raised, as we have seen, was essentially to say that it was all the people's fault. They had not kept the Covenant. The rulers, too, had not kept the Covenant or been properly responsible for the special gifts which they had from YHWH. Punishment was more or less inevitable and there was no putting it off with short-term political fixes. Only a massive religious realignment might work. Against this background of political anxiety, and the inevitable variety of religious interpretations of events, we have access to four traditions, 'the seventh-century prophets'. They are: Zephaniah, Nahum, Habakkuk and Jeremiah.

Zephaniah is probably the earliest of these, though canonically the last. It is usual to consider him as a presence in the earlier years of the King Josiah's reign, and certainly to place him before the reforms of 621. The book forms a good link between the eighth-century traditions of Amos or Micah and these new times. In the opening chapter the Amos picture of the Day of the Lord is called upon as the vehicle of a mighty judgement against Jerusalem. This is on account of the wickedness of the people of the city, but also on account of the corruption of true religion there (1.8f.). This theme is taken up again in 3.1–7 (cf. 3.4). The second chapter employs the now familiar device of a judgement against the nations, as a way of establishing YHWH's sovereignty. After all there isn't much point in being a prophet in these circumstances unless you speak for a God who can influence international events. A later addition, 3.8ff. – following a now familiar pattern – speaks of a return from exile and the preservation of a remnant (3.12f.). In the process we see the reworking of traditional theological themes about Zion (3.11ff.), and allusions to the God of the Exodus (3.17). The now familiar process of downfall and restoration is nowhere more succinctly expressed than in this book.

Reflection on text

Read Zephaniah 3.11–20. This oracle about restoration contains many, if not most, of the themes we see in other prophets. Look through the passage to see if you can identify these themes: remnant, Zion, exodus, covenant language about love, keeping law, kingship, the D theme of joy, gathering the dispersed.

Nahum is probably the next book in the historical sequence of the events that it is meant to be understood against. This book would certainly be a finalist in the 'least-read book of the Old Testament' competition. On the face of it, its reference is very specific, and the prophecy is not easily transported to some other time or circumstances. It is essentially a reaction to the downfall of Assyria in 612. The book is unusual in that it contains no judgement against Israel. To that extent its 'jingoistic' and apparently uncritical nationalism is both a surprise and a scandal. The book assumes that God is on side with Israel, and that this massive threat to Judah's security has somehow closed the book. 'Judah, though your punishment has been great, yet it will pass away and be gone. I have afflicted you, but I shall not afflict you again' (1.12, see also 1.15). The almost obscene pleasure the writer takes in the downfall of the enemy leaves the modern reader uncomfortable, and perhaps reluctant to accept sympathetic interpretations of its purpose in terms of God's sovereignty and his ability to punish wickedness (Achtemeier 1986, p. 6). Commentators also point to its place in the canon: next but one to Jonah and next to Habakkuk. Jonah deals specifically with the wickedness of Assyria. God sends Jonah to Nineveh to preach God's forgiveness following repentance. This is a message Jonah is unwilling to deliver. We see in Nahum the same sentiment that drives the vengeful Jonah. Jonah derives from post-exilic times and is the result of reflection in different theological times, but in the canon as we have it, the juxtaposition of these two is interesting.

Habakkuk is an altogether more rewarding book. This is a quieter reflection on events, dating from the last decade of the seventh century. This book is less concerned with the fall of Assyria than with the rise of Babylon. Structurally the book is interesting because it appears to make use of a number of liturgical fragments, but its main interest lies in its basic theological questioning about divine justice. Habakkuk is prepared to believe that Judah may be punished, but cannot see why the punishment should come from a nation that is more morally reprehensible than they. Chapter 1 introduces the subject of justice, and the main lament of Habakkuk (1.2–4). God's response is to describe how Babylon is being sent to punish Israel (1.6–11). Habakkuk then responds again with the main question: 'Why do you countenance the treachery of the wicked? Why keep silent when they devour those who are more righteous?' (1.13b). This is the unanswered question, but it becomes clear that for this writer, religious faith is not about having answers but about trusting. One of the Bible's greatest and most mature statements of such faith is to be found in 3.17f., a sentiment which is born of experience, and capable of application in many subsequent theological settings, as God's ways become even more inexplicable. Habakkuk sees that if the job of the prophet is to explain God in the face of disaster, then it is largely a lost cause. The prophet's job is to wait and trust.

Reflection on text

Read Habakkuk 3.17f. Why do you think this passage might be described as 'mature'?

But the major prophet of this period is **Jeremiah**. Older scholarship tended towards a biographical exegesis of the book, concentrating on Jeremiah's supposed membership of the Josiah reform party, and the implications of that for his own family life; since his father was in charge of one of the shrines Josiah had closed, and presumably at odds with the whole reform agenda. Commentators like Theodore Robinson drew attention to the similarities between Jeremiah and Hosea: how they both use similar relationship words to describe Israel and God, and to paint a picture of a lonely sensitive wronged man. More modern writers see the links with Hosea as establishing Jeremiah in the Sinai covenant tradition, and associating him with the D traditions of the north. However, the book does invite some biographical reflection, and that can be said legitimately to be part of its strategy. A series of 'confessions' or 'laments' in chapters 11—20 strike the modern reader as being rather like the 'video diary' sections of modern reality TV shows, where the main public narrative is interrupted to give an insight into the soul-searching of the protagonists. Examples are to be found at 11.18–23; 12.1–6; 15.10–12, 15–21; 17.14–18; 18.9–23; 20.7–11, 14–18. These are written with all the intensity of a video diary. 'I had been like a pet lamb led trustingly to the slaughter; I did not realize they were hatching plots against me and saying, "Let us destroy the tree while the sap is in it; let us cut him off from the land of the living, so that his name will be wholly forgotten"'(11.19).

For those who like to read the small print (as they say in the kind of adverts in holiday brochures which clearly hope that you won't want to find out just what a bum deal you've got) the book's structure is actually quite complicated and its provenance a matter of debate. Chapters 1—20 are commonly ascribed to the prophet Jeremiah, and deal with the crisis facing Jerusalem as Exile approaches. This is mirrored in chapters 37—45, which are a sustained historical narrative of the last days of Jerusalem. Chapters 46—51, which may have been displaced from their original setting in the book, are a series of oracles against the nations. Chapters 30—33 include the most striking message of hope for the future. Chapters 30 and 31 are sometimes known as the Book of Comfort, for that reason. There are other hints of new possibility in chapters 25 and 52. The book is a mixture of oracle and narrative. It is usually thought that the narrative is provided by D writers who carried Jeremiah's words with them into exile, but the exact relationship between the two is disputed.

For those who'd like to get a sense of the bigger picture, here are some of the broad-brush strokes.

Jeremiah paints a relentlessly realistic picture of exile. He paints a frightening and recognizable picture of what happens in communities consumed by anxiety, looking for scapegoats. He maintains the religious traditions which form part of the trajectory reaching back towards Hosea, and even the Mosaic traditions; about a God who is known and wants to be known and understood in relationship terms. He picks up one theological idea that is going to be very important in the continuing tradition – that of forgiveness – from Hosea (6.4) and works with it (5.7, 9; 9.9). One of the key themes for Jeremiah is the difference between truth and deception: between appearance and reality. Of the hundred or so occurrences of the Hebrew word for 'lie, deception' in the Old Testament, 35 are in Jeremiah. He is particularly scathing towards those who claim that peace is about to break out. He does not believe in quick fixes. This is not just a personal truth, but a national, public and political one. It is interesting that we have so much biographical narrative in which to situate this thinker. He is second only to Paul in the New Testament in that respect. (And in both cases that may be more to do with editorial intent than 'real' history.) The very word 'Jeremiah' has come to epitomize, in English idiom, someone who is mournful and whose glass is always half empty when everyone else's is half full. This is unfair. His mission was to a people clinging to an unsustainable and totally fantastic optimism, failing to face up to reality, and wanting not to hear the truth. Jeremiah was vindicated in that what he prophesied happened. And the hope which his book contains, includes the theological seeds which we shall see blossom in later tradition.

Reflection on text

Read Jeremiah 7.1–11. This is part of a 'sermon' delivered by Jeremiah on the steps of the temple. Now read Matthew 7.21–3, and Matthew 21.12f. These are reported words of Jesus, the latter also delivered in the temple. What light (if any) does each passage throw on the other?

The prophet **Ezekiel** is normally classed as a prophet of the sixth century or a prophet of the Exile, so you might expect him to come in the next chapter, and indeed he could, but in important respects he belongs with Jeremiah. His prophecy is precisely dated to 593 (1.2), which places him just a few years after Jeremiah. Moreover he is located, at this time, with the first body of exiles removed from Jerusalem in 597. His reflections stand alongside those of Jeremiah, then, in terms of time, place and context. But just as the connections from Jeremiah lead us towards the D traditions of the Old Testament – the D way of making sense of what has happened and the D way of prescribing how the future can be made safe and religiously meaningful – so

Ezekiel connects us with the P traditions of making sense and the P way of making safe and meaningful. And so for Ezekiel we find a preoccupation with holiness and purity; and with how those have been compromised and subverted. This subversion has involved crossing the boundaries that are key to the preservation of order in the P tradition. His vision of the future is couched in terms of a new temple: an idiom which will find fuller expression in the New Testament in 1 Peter and ultimately in the book of Revelation. His prescription involves a newly consecrated people. This message is set in the familiar scheme of judgement and downfall, on the one hand; and new life and restoration on the other. Conveniently, the book divides into two roughly equal halves, each half dealing with one of the themes. Chapters 1—24 deal with downfall and 25—48 with restoration.

A case could equally well be made for discussing Ezekiel alongside the figure referred to traditionally as 2 Isaiah, the other major prophet of the Exile. The most striking similarity between them is that they both have to deal with the new crisis about God. This crisis arises as soon as the community is separated from the land. The question is how and whether the God of Israel can be present and effective without a land of his own. 2 Isaiah deals with this, in terms of a creation theology that we shall look at elsewhere. Ezekiel develops the idea of sacramental presence, which assumes that God can be present, given certain circumstances, despite the geographical location. Those circumstances are to do with ritual and holiness, and hence seem somewhat esoteric to us now.

Just as Jeremiah has attracted exegesis fascinated by the biographical data supplied in his book, so older commentators have been fascinated by the man Ezekiel. His book records some of the more bizarre acts among the prophets. Some of his passion and venom verges on the pornographic in its intensity. Some of the visions are truly fantastic. Ezekiel has in the past been diagnosed as psychotic, schizophrenic and paranoid. More modern assessments do not go there. He is neither mad nor bad nor sad; he is just reacting to experience using the theological tools at his disposal, and the theological imagination which belongs to his call. In some respects we can see echoes of Jeremiah. Chapter 13, for example, condemns those who preach a false peace. But the imagery employed by Ezekiel to describe the way in which the people of Israel have lost their innocence and potential for holiness is quite different from Jeremiah's: heavy with sexual allegory, which is chilling in its detailed working out (see chapters 16 and 23 for example). Equally involved and detailed is the vision of the future; whether that be in the visions of the new temple, in chapters 40—48, or the apocalyptic visions of chapters 39 and 40, or in the series of allegorical reflections about the restored Israel, the most famous of which is the 'dry bones' vision of chapter 37.

Reflection on text

Read Ezekiel 23.1–21. This is unlikely to be a portion of the book that you've heard read aloud anywhere, unlike, perhaps, the vision of the dry bones, but it is still part of the biblical canon. In the passage the author uses extended reference to sexual imagery to describe the downfall of both the northern and southern kingdoms. How legitimate do you think this is? What questions does it raise for you in the reading of this prophet?

The prophets whose words are set in the years leading towards exile (and whose books will be editorially constructed from that perspective) have in common the task of theological reflection. They bring together an astute awareness of their present context and their understanding of the various traditions of YHWH religion in which they stand, in a way which enables each to work on the other and make this one of the truly creative theological periods in the history of the canon. The two main traditions of D and P represent different responses to the crisis, but it is the achievement of the canon process that they stand in the Bible side by side. The questions that are posed in the face of the kind of disaster that calls God's nature, integrity, even his existence into question, are still with us, and the alternative answers are still recognizable, as are the different forms of religious life which spring from them. That is a theme to which we shall return.

12

Beyond Blame

In describing Ezekiel alongside prophets of the seventh century, we have strayed a little from convention. In this chapter we shall stray even further by describing prophets of the Exile alongside the so-called prophets of the Return. The major difference between the books we have discussed and those in this chapter, is that the theological reflections of the former deal largely with the question, 'How could God let this (Exile disaster) happen?' From now on, the reflections will centre on the theme, 'What does, and will it mean, to be the people of God in the future?' To be sure, the theme of restoration has been evident till now, though the situation is complicated by scholars' belief that some of the restoration oracles in those books actually date from this Exile or post-Exile period. But from now on we move beyond blame. The creative theology occasioned by the crises of the seventh century has given new material on which to reflect. It has become possible to think and articulate new things about God, born of the experience of abandonment and loss, on the one hand; and the experience of finding God in new places, speaking in new ways, on the other. The most exciting evidence of what is new is provided by a writer in the Isaiah tradition, conventionally known as **2 Isaiah**, and responsible for chapters 40—55 of that book.

Reflection on experience

We are beginning to see the emergence of two different approaches to religious life. One reflects on past sin and present forgiveness; the other on the present as a time of opportunity to move forward towards a new vision in hope. To which of these are you instinctively drawn? Do you have any experience of faith communities which might illustrate the differences?

The psychological shift from Isaiah chapter 39 to chapter 40 is perhaps best described as like two musical movements in a symphony. The two sections of the book are related and recognizably so, but a completely new style takes up the underlying theme of judgement and restoration, and replays it with different instrumentation. In this 'second movement' of Isaiah everything changes. There is a new majesty in the poetry and a new setting for it. YHWH summons his accusers to court and puts his case with a new rhetoric (41.1; 43.8–12; 45.20f.). Opposing gods and systems are refuted contemptuously (41.22–4; 46.1f.). There is a new confidence as even satire is employed to demonstrate just how pathetic is the power of these imposter gods (44.14–20). There is a new message of comfort in place of punishment (40.1; 43.18f.; 51.12) and a new declaration of the relationship between YHWH and his people (41.8–10; 42.6–9; 44.1–5; 52.7–10). This is in part occasioned by a new more realistic hope. The generalized message of restoration of earlier prophets is now given political shape to become more like a divine strategy. The power of Babylon is on the decline (chapter 47). Cyrus the Persian, Cyrus the Kurd, is the new name on the block. He it is who in just a couple of years after this writing, in 538, will defeat the might of Babylon in a bloodless coup, opening the way for a new edict, which will allow those Judaeans who wish to do so to return to their former land. The astonishing thing is that YHWH is proclaimed, by Isaiah, as the designer of this history. Cyrus is not just a convenient political saviour. He is the servant of YHWH and is described as such with vigour in 44.21—45.7. YHWH confides in him, speaks to him directly, and inspires him. This is as remarkable as a Christian writer today describing some great Jewish, Muslim or Chinese leader as God's servant and confidante, in the modern world. But this strategy is couched in the theological language of exodus. This will mean a new journey through the wilderness (40.3), where they will be miraculously cared for, as in the first Exodus (41.17–20; 43.16f.; 48.20–2).

Reflection on text

Read Isaiah 44.14–20. This is a very well written piece of satire about idol-worshippers, which may well have a 'modern' feel to you, compared with some of the other things you've read. Could you imagine rewriting it for a modern situation?

All of this is possible only because of a new theological understanding, which the experience of exile has taught the people. The crisis of exile was a crisis, in the first place, of *presence*. How could the God of Israel be present in a foreign jurisdiction? The old understanding of the boundaries of God is quaintly expressed in 2 Kings 5, where Naaman the Syrian, having been miraculously cured of his leprosy wants to take two buckets of Israelite soil home with him so that he can continue to worship YHWH there. The implication is that it is only possible to worship the God of Israel on Israelite soil. YHWH is a great god, the best god even, but he is one among many. Israel is lucky to have him, and he is better than other countries' gods. The new theological understanding is that in fact there is but one God who bestrides human boundaries, and is as able to influence the lives of his people in Babylon as he is in Israel. The second crisis of exile is about the *power* of God. 2 Isaiah contains some of the strongest statements anywhere in the Old Testament about YHWH's ability to influence events, using the rhetoric of a God who is alone able to create. The third crisis of exile is about God's *will and intention*. Does he still love his people? Does he want to maintain relationship with them? In passionate language, the answer is yes.

This new theological understanding has implications. These could perhaps be expressed in three sentences as follows.

- If YHWH is the one God, then he must be God of all creation.
- If YHWH is the one God he must be God of all history.
- If YHWH is the one God he must be God of all peoples.

Although evidenced in 2 Isaiah, the exploration of the first of these statements about God will become the concern of the wisdom literature, so-called. The exploration of the second will give rise to the genre of apocalyptic writing. The exploration of the third will be reflected in writings such as the books of Jonah and Ruth. These new 'discoveries' about God, these new sightings or revelations about God, will lead to the kind of theological reflection that will determine the theological agenda of the people of YHWH for hundreds of years. The theological understanding brings with it a new sense of the vocation of Israel.

Within 2 Isaiah there are four passages about vocation, which have occasioned much scholarly debate (42.1–9; 49.1–6; 50.4–9; 52.13—53.12). These four poems are sometimes called the 'servant songs' or the 'songs of the suffering servant' because each of them describes a servant who through suffering will bring about a better state of affairs. That is: the servant's suffering will be for a purpose; it will be redemptive.

Reflection on text

Read Isaiah 49.1–6. This is the second of the servant songs. Note in verse 4 the reference to 'suffering'. Clearly the author feels something he has done is in vain. To what extent does the song express something you are familiar with? What kind of sympathy do you have for the proposed solution: that this is all part of God's bigger purpose?

The songs have sustained scholarly interest because of the place they have had in the subsequent (Christian) tradition. Clearly, poems in the tradition which describe how suffering, ordained by God, can be of benefit, and can represent a triumph rather than a disaster, are going to be important for the first Christians, trying to make sense of the death of Jesus. And so it proves. From the perspective of Old Testament scholarship there has been much debate about the identity of this anonymous servant. He has been regarded variously as Cyrus, Moses, Hezekiah, the embodiment of Israel, or even, disregarding contemporary reference in favour of a future prophetic one, Jesus. The current consensus is around the idea that the author uses the term 'servant' consistently to mean Israel, though it is recognized that 49.6 does create something of a problem for that interpretation. Brueggemann argues that this new vocation for Israel is effectively a restatement of the vocational declaration in Genesis 12.3. But the newness of the context is provided by the introduction of the concept of suffering.

We shall look at this in more detail as we consider the wisdom writings, but it is worth marking here that the problem of suffering takes on a new dimension as a result of the new theological statements which 2 Isaiah is beginning to articulate. It is one thing to be bowled over by the power and might of a God who can create worlds and nations, and order history. But soon the collision of faith and experience prompts the question, 'Why did God create or organize the world thus?' And that inevitably leads to questions about suffering, which are addressed by the wisdom writers as well as here. If God is so great and loving and powerful, why is there disease, warfare, waste of resources and death? 2 Isaiah does not give complete answers to any of these questions, but begins, rather, to give permission for them to be asked. And all of this is regarded as something new, and as such it is good news. Words derived from the Hebrew root *basar*, to bear good tidings, are used by 2 Isaiah at 40.9; 41.27 and 52.7, in a way that prefigures the use of the word 'gospel' by early Christian writers. Here is a series of completely new theological possibilities opened up as the result of a new sighting of, a new revelation from, a new realization about, God. That is the crucial importance of this innovative second movement of Isaiah.

There is a third movement. Scholars refer to it as Third Isaiah or **3 Isaiah**, and it consists of chapters 56—66. The theme of good news is carried forward (60.6 and 61.1, which imitates the style of the servant songs, and is familiar from its quotation in Luke's Gospel 4.18f.), but actually the news is different as the context has changed. These oracles, which may not all have the same author, are set in the period of restoration after the Return. It is perhaps worth noting that one huge issue for the people of Judah must have been whether to return or not. As far as the Old Testament is concerned, the history of the people of YHWH is maintained by those who do return. But having returned, as the accompanying historical account bears witness (see Chapter 17) the lofty vision of 2 Isaiah translates all too quickly into mundane reality. The kinds of issue that are now top of the list are to do with identity. Once the questions about blame and fault had been met with the new word of forgiveness and comfort, the questions were all about 'What does, and will it mean, to be the people of God in the future?' And to find an answer, the people turned to what had sustained their identity in the exile period.

And so, marks of distinctiveness such as the institutions of religion, the observance of the sabbath, and male circumcision, became important areas for debate. The familiar P concerns about purity and boundaries are never far away, occasioned perhaps by intermarriage, or by fellow travellers, taking their chance with the returning Israelites. These are familiar questions in the modern world as well, and we can identify easily with them. At a banal level, who has the right to play football for their country? Must you be born there? What if you're not born there but your parents were, or perhaps just one parent is enough, or perhaps even a grandparent? Or could you play for your country if you have no blood tie to the place but you've lived there for a length of time? How long should that be? And what if you're the child of immigrants with a name which is culturally quite different from native names: does that disqualify you? At a more political level: what gives a person the right to a passport? And with echoes of the Old Testament, who should be counted as citizens of the post-1948 state of Israel? This is the background to the issues which we begin to see emerge in 3 Isaiah.

Chapter 56, for example is about how you define inclusiveness.

Reflection on text

Read Isaiah 56.1–8. Having read some of the P theology which emphasizes boundaries and purity, does this come as a bit of a surprise? Which do you think is the most modern, or the most appropriate in your own circumstances? What do you think might have occasioned the shift in this writer?

Chapter 58 raises issues about what constitutes a proper 'fast'. We might imagine a fairly heated debate here between those who want simply to observe rituals, and those who want to see the spiritual heart and meaning of the ritual as more important (58.3–7). This discussion leads into one about the sabbath (58.13f.) about which there seems no such controversy. Chapters 60—62 offer an interlude of more inspirational poetry akin to that of 2 Isaiah, and highlighting the importance of Jerusalem, but disillusion about the actual state of affairs in Jerusalem is never far away (chapter 64) and gives rise eventually to a new expectation (chapters 65, 66). It's as if the people are asking (echoing the title of Bob Geldof's autobiography), Is That It? The inspirational message about the power, the intent and the vocation of this international God surely meant more than coming to a set of ruins in the middle of nowhere. And so in another burst of theological creativity we see the prophets of the period beginning to reflect anew theologically, using now, not only the themes of the Exodus in which to couch their message, but also those of Return and Restoration, particularly focusing on Jerusalem.

Scholars employing the critical methods used by historians have found rich pickings in Isaiah, with its mixture of authors, dates, literary genres and traditions. The importance of passages used by later theologians of the New Testament period have also encouraged scholars to make detailed study of specific texts. More recently, as literary approaches have begun to make an impact, it has become more common for scholars to look for unifying themes and trends in the book of Isaiah as a whole, while bearing in mind the conclusions of former historical study. It is clear that the typical prophetic theme of downfall and restoration is echoed in Isaiah. (Indeed there may be a third category – Reorganization (so Brueggemann 2003, p. 171), though the text does not demand it.) It is clear also that this theme is echoed in that of judgement and hope, which accompanies it in other prophetic books. What is distinctive here, though, is the centrality of Jerusalem. Brueggemann believes that, in this respect, 1.21–7 acts as an overture to the theme of the whole book. What is also distinctive is the grappling with the question, 'What does it mean to be the people of God in these new circumstances?'

The post-exilic period is sometimes thought to be a rather thin period for theology but that would be to do it an injustice. It is to this period which scholars are now looking as, in a sense, the most creative period of all – the time when the final edition of the Old Testament begins to take form. The materials used for the theological reflections thus fashioned may belong to a different age, but the reflections themselves are innovative and daring. They are carried out against the background of the issues set out for us by Isaiah, and in the realization, in particular, that new theological work is now possible, and in a sense necessary, as a result of the new things about God which the Exile had revealed.

3 Isaiah is not the only post-exilic prophetic voice. We can conclude our survey of the prophetic books by looking at the others. In Chapter 17 we shall look at the historical commentary meant to accompany all this, 1 and 2 Chronicles, Ezra and Nehemiah. Suffice it to say here that three of the Book of the Twelve Prophets, Haggai, Zechariah and Malachi, are conventionally dated to the beginning of the so-called Persian period, after the Edict of Cyrus in 538, and prior to the completion of the second Jerusalem temple in

around 515. During this period, Judaea was a small client state of the Persian empire, useful to the empire because it opened the way to more powerful Egypt. An issue in these early years was the relationship between Judah and Samaria, which had been controlling the former Judaean territory. In fact complete independence from Samaria was not accomplished for almost a hundred years. The Persian period itself lasted until defeat by Alexander the Greek in 333 BCE.

Haggai, dated to the time of Darius, 520–516, consists of four main oracles, three of which express a very priestly understanding of how well-being is to return to the community, and how its identity is to be defined. The picture we infer from this book is of a marginal demoralized community, disappointed in their grand hopes for the Return. In this they are not unlike very many peoples who set off for what is in effect virgin territory with great hopes for a better life, only to find that reality does not match the dream. Haggai's message is that the temple must be built in order for prosperity to return. Ritual purity can thus be restored. Drought and disaster will follow inactivity (1.10f.). We also see a picture of a society that is dominated more by priests (2.10–14). The fourth oracle (2.20–3) has a more eschatological feel: that is, it looks beyond the immediate unfolding of history to a more direct intervention of God in history which will change the course of things and allow the ultimate destiny of the people to be realized. We shall deal with this kind of theme in Chapter 14. Noteworthy here is the particular vehicle for this theology, which is couched in terms of the establishment of a new Jerusalem, or Davidic dispensation.

Zechariah 1—8 belongs to this period, dated very close to Haggai. It contains a series of skilful (literary) visions, such as the golden lampstand (4.1–7) and the four chariots (6.1–8). 6.11–14 also gives the priests the key role in restoration. Jerusalem is important here as in Haggai. 8.8 includes a covenant formula, and may show knowledge of Jeremiah. In any case this book is closer to pre-exilic prophecy than Haggai. When the collection of prophets was first made, Zechariah was the last named prophet. It was followed by three anonymous collections of oracles which can now be read as Zechariah 9—11 and 12—14, and then **Malachi.** 'Malachi' is a transliteration of Hebrew words from the anonymous oracle, meaning 'my messenger'. The remaining oracles of Zechariah and Malachi continue to assume a priestly context. Malachi includes an interesting literary device – a series of argument dialogues which carry the message forward. The reference at the end of the book to Elijah (4.5) provides a convenient link to the New Testament which follows it in Christian Bibles, as John the Baptist is portrayed as a second Elijah. It is likely that the books **Obadiah** and **Joel** can also be dated to this period.

The message of the post-exilic prophets is addressed to a quite specific context. It is important to note that the new theological agenda set out by 2 Isaiah is being addressed in other places (as we shall see) and that this is not 'all there is'. However, there are some common themes in this writing which do make their contribution to the development of theology.

- There is a common belief that judgement is past and that a new age is dawning. Zechariah 8.4 compares with Isaiah 2.4 and Micah 4.4. YHWH's 'anger' is still real though now directed much more towards the nations (Zechariah 1.15).
- In these books, it is clear that salvation is to be appropriated through the life of the temple and all that that involves in terms of a vision of life in which purity and the maintenance of boundaries will best honour YHWH's presence and keep the world safe. The new Israel is presented therefore as a theocratic community, headed by priests.
- The people are characteristically referred to as a 'remnant'. A remnant is 'what is left', and that can be either a negative or a comforting idea. 'There will hardly been anything left' is the very threatening use of the term in, for example, Amos 3.12. Here, though, the term has the sense of 'You alone have been spared'. This is part of the quest for definition and identity among the people, and as such is a very exclusive term. These are now the only legitimate heirs of promise: the only legitimate interpreters of tradition (Haggai 1.12–14; 2.2; Zecharaiah 8.6–12). The term will continue to be important in expressions of religious faith, which are sectarian and exclusive.
- The way is clear for a theology of the nation's ultimate destiny which uses the traditions of Jerusalem as key media. We shall consider this further in Chapter 14.

CHAPTER 13 SUMMARY

What is this chapter about?

This chapter is the first of a series which looks, in a thematic way, at the theological implications of the Exile. This first looks at creation theology, and includes description and discussion of the contents of Proverbs.

What books are referred to?

Robert Alter, 'The poetic and wisdom books', in John Barton (ed.), *The Cambridge Companion to Biblical Interpretation* (Cambridge: Cambridge University Press, 1998), pp. 226–40.

What other books would be helpful?

You may well discover that complete books dealing with this area are difficult to find. Some will seem dated and others inaccessible. An exception on creation issues generally is Bernhard W. Anderson, *From Creation to New Creation: Old Testament Perspectives* (Minneapolis: Fortress Press, 1994). Brueggemann's commentary on Genesis in the Interpretation series (Atlanta: John Knox Press, 1982) is also readable and helpful.

How is the chapter organized?

An introduction defining the term 'creation theology', and setting it in an Old Testament context, is followed by a description of the book of Proverbs that illustrates its main characteristics. There is further initial discussion on the other wisdom books, followed by a more detailed résumé of Proverbs. Finally there is a brief discussion linking Proverbs with other wisdom material.

What should I be able to do by the end of this chapter?

Recount the main characteristics of creation theology.

Relate them to biblical texts.

Describe the main features of the book of Proverbs.

13

First Things Last

The experience of exile was a profound theological shock to the adherents of the religion of YHWH. Either they had to abandon YHWH or they had to rethink a great deal of what they had thought they knew for certain about him. Our Old Testament is the record of those who took the latter course. That process of rethinking had a negative aspect: How could God let this happen? It also had a positive aspect in that new and wondrous things had in effect been discovered about God. Whereas, before the Exile, YHWH had been considered a national God, one among many, albeit able to hold his own against the rest, now he was clearly supranational, able to determine international events in history. It was a short step from this kind of thinking to the monotheism that we see being developed in 2 Isaiah. That monotheism, as we have seen, occasioned new flights of theological imagination. And one of them was the thesis that if YHWH is the only God then he must be God of all creation. A whole new strand of theological thinking was thus born.

Reflection on experience

What would you expect to be the main differences for a faith community whose idea of God changes from being the god of a particular locality, or perhaps a 'themed' god (e.g. god of fertility), to being a universal God of the kind we begin to see envisaged here? Having read the chapter and the texts, see if your hunches prove correct.

Other considerations contributed to its form.

- The Babylonians already had a creation theology, so some cultural factors may have been important here. Older commentators spent a great deal of time considering the relationship between Babylonian creation myths and the accounts in Genesis 1—5, and while this is not currently in vogue it has validity. Some more modern commentators (such as Brueggemann, in *Genesis* (1982) see in the Genesis accounts a conscious attempt to develop an alternative theology to that of Babylon (which is one way of saying that the context of Babylon contributed to the development of the theology).
- After the Exile, questions of vocation and identity were top of the agenda. What does it mean to be a follower of YHWH? What does it mean to be an Israelite or a Jew? How shall we maintain our distinctiveness? Does God still have some role for Israel in the unfolding history of the world? Such questions, in many cultures, are addressed in creation stories that describe the nation's or the tribe's distinctiveness and purpose. This was an appropriate medium in which to answer these questions for those reflecting post-Exile.

Creation theologies do not attempt to answer questions about how the world was created. They are about subsequent relations in the created order. Questions around:

- The relation between men and women;
- The relation between different nations;
- The relation between humankind and God;
- The relation between humankind and the wider environment;
- The means of resolution of conflict and maintenance of peace;
- The boundaries that affect human life;

are the kinds of questions with which such theology deals. In the Old Testament we see the movement towards creation theology in 2 Isaiah. We see explicit examples of creation theology at the beginning of Genesis, and we see some reflections on, and applications of, creation theology in the Psalms.

Reflection on text

Read the first two creation accounts in Genesis 1, and Genesis 2.4ff. Do you see the bulleted points above reflected in these accounts? Are there other themes not mentioned here? Is this a new way for you of looking at these kinds of writing? If so, how does that affect the way you read?

There is a particular relationship between creation theology and the so-called **Wisdom Literature.** This literature consists of the books of Proverbs, Job and Ecclesiastes, within the main Old Testament canon, though, like apocalyptic literature, there is development in the inter-testamental period, as well as scattered evidence of the genre in other parts of the Old Testament – most notably in the Psalms. Rather confusingly, in modern Christian Bibles, these three main books are arranged in the canon in a way that does not make their relationship either to each other or to other literature at all clear. It is usually assumed that **Proverbs** is the oldest of the books, or at least, that it contains the oldest material. In its final form it owes much to editorial composition. Different sources are acknowledged and obvious. The book consists of wise sayings suitable for teaching young men about the world, human society and appropriate behaviour. The main contents of the book include chapters 1—9, which is the main theological section, the proverbs of Solomon (10.1—22.16), and words attributed to the 'men of Hezekiah' (chapters 25—29), as well as shorter sections credited to a variety of wise sources.

While there is general agreement that the finished book is a product of early post-exilic Judaism, there is little agreement about the original context of the sayings or indeed the context of the editors. It may be that some of the sayings are ancient and have their origins in the family group, as part of traditional parenting. At this stage the material would have been passed on in oral tradition. The question of who wrote it down and when is more difficult. It may be, also, that some of the material derives from a 'school' context. Proverbs 22.17—24.22, for example, resembles closely the Egyptian 'Instruction of Amenemope', a school text. But it does not follow that just because material was used in a school setting in Egypt it was used similarly in Judaea. The intellectual activity reflected in the sayings suggests a context that at some stage involved an intellectual elite of some kind. The temple and the court have been suggested as (the only such) possibilities. The traditional link with Solomon has pointed scholars towards the court of Solomon as a centre for this intellectual energy, and the thesis that there was some kind of renaissance at that court has been popular for some time; though it has to be said that there is little solid evidence for this or indeed any other solution to the problem. It is likely that no tidy solution is possible and that we have to accept that the sayings derived from lots of contexts over a long period. The evidence of widespread wisdom material in the Psalms supports this view. This conclusion, of course, has the effect of concentrating the theological interest in the time of the editors of Proverbs. Why did they collect this material and publish it? What theological position did it derive from? That is where the post-exilic interest in creation theology has importance, since that is the most obvious theological home for these writings.

The theological argument for the integrity of these writings is that if there is one God who is creator of all and who has purpose for all, then it should be possible to discern the hand of the creator in the creation. By observing the world closely, we are able to find hints and allusions, and more than that, rules and axioms, which will tell us something more about God's purpose and nature, as well as telling us about what it means to be truly human and truly at home in the world which God has created. What we see here is an alternative to the means of accessing information about God provided by the Covenant tradition. That tradition saw God at his most creative in the midst of the political process, speaking directly to historic contexts through historic figures. This tradition sees access to information about God being provided by observation of the natural world, and in particular, observation of human behaviour and its consequences. This is different also from the post-exilic apocalyptic tradition (see Chapter 14) with which some have sought to compare it. The wisdom tradition seeks the answers to the questions about creation, and seeks to unravel the mysteries of creation, through what is self-evident rather than by special revelation. Both Covenant and Wisdom traditions resource ethical consideration. The one might be called revealed theology: the other natural theology. Both have a long history of coexistence in the Christian tradition in particular. The wisdom approach is closely linked to what we would call scientific method, and particularly social scientific method, where conclusions are based on case studies of human relations. The point is sometimes made that it is through gathering this literature together, and engaging in this kind of intellectual reflection on reality, that the Old Testament writers 'came of age' within an intellectual culture which spans most of the rest of the ancient world at that time.

It is central to the wisdom writings in Proverbs that acts have consequences, and that choices must be made. Commonly the choice is between walking in one of two ways, which are contrasted as to their outcome (e.g. 4.10–19; 12.28). Underlying this quest lies the belief that 'Someone who is clever will have the wit to find the right way; the folly of the stupid misleads them' (14.8). Even more fundamentally, 'The fear of the Lord is the foundation of knowledge; it is fools who scorn wisdom and instruction' (1.7). When combined with ethical instruction in this way, creation theology has particular characteristics.

It is innately *conservative*. It takes the 'ought' of life from the 'is' and has no dynamic for change. It carries an assumption that the blueprint for human behaviour has been laid down in some eternal way, from creation, and that it simply needs to be learned. It is somewhat *naive*, particularly in its treatment of good and evil, as if they were always self-evident, and as if choices were always between clearly defined options with inevitable outcomes (20.7). There is no moral maze here. Life is essentially a simple matter. Added to this, Proverbs is the most *optimistic* of the wisdom writings. A full and happy life is possible and attainable (3.2; 4.10; 14.27), a view expressed simply yet fully at 19.23, 'The fear of the Lord is life; he who is full of it will rest untouched by evil.' It is *institutional* in two ways. First, it is rule-bound. All life operates by rules and axioms whose outcomes are demonstrable. Learning to be fully human actually means learning and keeping the rules. Second, it accepts the role of institutions within life, which are themselves governed by rules (e.g. family/marriage). Nevertheless – and particularly in contrast to what can seem like the rather arid works of the P writers, or the deep poetry of prophetic oracle or more considered wisdom writing such as is found in Job – these writings in proverbs are both *accessible* and interestingly attractive. They demonstrate an excellent understanding of teaching method and communication generally. These writings include more humour than most of the rest of the Old Testament. One example of many is 30.29. 'Three things there are which are stately in their stride, four which are stately as they move: the lion, mighty among beasts, which will not turn tail for anyone; the strutting cock; the he-goat; and a king going forth at the head of his army.'

Reflection on text

Read Proverbs 14. This is a typical example of much of the book. Can you see the characteristics outlined above in this passage? What is your response to the fact that God doesn't put in much of an appearance here?

Later wisdom writings, later reflections on life, take a different and more subversive view, as we shall see. The observations that are made here are from the perspective of the successful – as we might imagine an intellectual elite to be. (Here is ample material for a hermeneutic of suspicion.) There is no opportunity in these writings to reflect on what happens when the rules will not bear the weight placed on them. What, for example, is to be said when someone keeps all the rules but does not prosper? This too can be observed, but it is left to the book of Job to deal with the implications of such observation. Ecclesiastes, with different material and from a different perspective also challenges the institutional optimism of Proverbs. That is not to say that the understanding of religious life exemplified in Proverbs is long-since extinct. Indeed, far from it. Many would recognize key elements of the wisdom world-view in much current religious practice.

A good place to begin to understand this world-view is actually in the book of Job, chapter 31. Here Job is pleading his case to be regarded as a worthy person. He describes conduct that a person schooled in the Proverbs world-view would regard as reprehensible, and says, in effect, 'I didn't do that.' From that chapter we can therefore build a picture of what a worthy, wise person (and by implication, one who would then expect to be rewarded with measurable success) would be like. A picture emerges of someone who is in all respects a good citizen. His word is dependable, he is faithful to his wife, he upholds justice, he has compassion on the poor, he honours ecological concerns, he fulfils the rules of hospitality and does not gossip. Queen Victoria would have been proud of him.

From further study of Proverbs itself, it is possible to add flesh to these bones and to discern the key elements of this world-view. It has these characteristics.

- Egocentricity is not at odds with spiritual devotion. It is quite all right to be concerned about, even centred on, 'me'.
- Social justice however is also important, particularly in the administration of justice (19.9) and the relief of need (14.21).
- The outward and accepted marks of human success – to be healthy, to be wealthy, to be well regarded (22.1) – are actually marks of God's favour. They demonstrate the advantages of co-operation with God.
- Family is the most important institution in society (20.20; 17.6). It follows that anything which undermines family life is seen as most threatening. 23.22–8 is a typical passage in which the son is urged to make his parents proud, immediately followed by a warning against adultery or prostitution.
- There is no dichotomy between the sacred and the secular. In effect all is sacred, because all has been created by God for a purpose.
- The main prize, apart from success in human terms, is actually to be alive. Life itself is the chief good, and aim of human striving. It follows then that death is something of a taboo. The path that is to be followed inevitably leads to life. Death is a kind of punishment (21.16).
- Discipline is important in all things. There must be a disciplined approach to the world of work (24.30–4; 10.4f.). There must be discipline within marriage (30.20), and children themselves must be disciplined either through verbal reproof (15.32; 12.1), or through a good beating (13.24; 20.30 and 23.13f.).
- All of this should lead to self-control, the real sign of maturity (25.21; 16.32).
- The place of women is rather ambiguous. Women are seen on the whole very much as adjuncts to men (18.22: thing?!). Yet wisdom personified, found in chapter 8 (although contrasted with the foolish woman of chapter 9), is female.

Reflection on text

Looking through the examples above, how much sense do you think it makes to adopt them as useful guidelines for life today? Are they universal truths or are they perhaps only useful in the culture which produced them? Do you think you might need to be aware of the underlying theological agenda in order to make sense of them as a moral code for today?

The wise man is constantly contrasted with the fool. There are eight different terms for 'fool' in Proverbs.

To round the picture off we might look at the things that are said to lead to destruction.

- The foremost of these is the adultress. 7.5–23 is a remarkably long cautionary tale. It purports to be something observed from a window, but the detail of the dialogue and the passion of the delivery makes that unlikely. Indeed it is expressed in terms that could almost be called erotic: 'Come let us drown ourselves in pleasure, let us abandon ourselves to a night of love,' says the adultress. If most sons heard this kind of thing from their father, they'd begin to wonder what the old boy's sources were! A similarly lengthy warning against adultery is to be found at 6.27–35.
- Also to be avoided is drunkenness. 23.29–35 is a description of drunkenness with which many students of my acquaintance can identify readily! The problem with drunkenness is that self-control is lost.
- Idleness (6.10) is to be despised.
- Loose talk is also problematic. Gossip is always wrong (18.8). It is usually right for a person to listen rather than speak (17.27f.).
- The real give-away for a person who has not exhibited wisdom is that he will have a nagging wife (27.15f.).

It is usual for Old Testament Introductions to spend very little time on Proverbs, and to be quite dismissive of any theological value in the book. Speaking of the wisdom literature in general Alter can write: '[the hortatory function] sets the wisdom books apart from the rest of biblical literature, and, as scholarship has long recognized, makes them the most international in character in the whole biblical corpus. The usual scriptural focus on the distinctiveness of Israel and its covenantal relationship with God is entirely absent; revelation and, arguably, theological perspectives are not much in evidence' (Alter 1998, pp. 232f.). Against this view it can be argued:

- These books, and Proverbs in particular, demonstrate a particular theology in action. They are an outworking and an exploration of what it might mean to regard one god as the God of all creation. In fact they are full of theological assertion, as the sustained attack on what Proverbs asserts, mounted by the author of the book of Job, surely proves.
- These proverbs are much more than common sense. Through creation theology they do give a distinctive local character to the international genre. The fear of the Lord is the beginning of wisdom.
- It is true that these sayings are not historically contextualized, but in a sense that gives them even greater theological force, in that the writer is making universal claims for his observations, based on a belief that YHWH is the one creator God.
- To regard only those portions of the Old Testament as authentic which deal with covenantal theology is to fall prey to all the objections which were made to Eichrodt's approach to the theology of the Old Testament a hundred years ago.

Two other observations might be made before we look at the subversive demolition of what Proverbs asserts about God and his ways, to be found in Job and Ecclesiastes. The first is that though there may be little here about the darker and more serious side of life, in common with the creation account of P in Genesis 1, there is something delightful about the positive view of creation set out. This is world-affirming stuff, which delights in right relations being honoured and believes that in the end all will be well and all manner of things shall be well, and that needs to be remembered. Second, building on the personification of Wisdom in Proverbs 8.22–31, and the close link between that figure, creation, and God himself ('I was at his side each day, his darling and delight, playing in his presence continually, playing over his whole world, while my delight was in mankind' – 8.30f.), there is a Christian interest in the links with wisdom in the New Testament, and especially with John 1.1–3. Was Jesus Wisdom made flesh?

The main problem with theology generally in its first post-exilic articulation was that it saw God as a great organizer, of the world and human history, who was almost too bound by the inevitability of his own design. There was insufficient room for mystery, for the freedom and continuing creativity of God, and too little attention paid to the complicated nature of the human condition. It was left to later wisdom writers, a later generation of intellectuals, to move the argument on.

CHAPTER 14 SUMMARY

What is this chapter about?

This chapter examines another theological development which occurs after the Exile, and results from that experience, namely, eschatology, the study of God's role in relation to history and destiny. Particular attention is paid to the genre of apocalyptic writing. The book of Daniel is cited as the main Old Testament example.

What books are referred to?

Donald Gowan, *Eschatology in the Old Testament* (Edinburgh: T & T Clark, 2000).

What other books would be helpful?

Many books are available on apocalyptic generally. The classic is D. S. Russell, *The Method and Message of Jewish Apocalyptic* (London: SCM Press, 1964). A more recent digest by the same author is *Divine Disclosure* (London: SCM Press, 1992). A good recent commentary on Daniel is also by Donald Gowan in the Abingdon series (Nashville: Abingdon Press, 2001).

How is the chapter organized?

An introduction locates the subject among the developments in post-exilic Old Testament theology. Thereafter these topics are investigated: the literary characteristics of apocalyptic; the theological characteristics of apocalyptic; the relation between the literature and its social context; Gowan's analysis of the overall scheme of Old Testament eschatology.

What should I be able to do by the end of this chapter?

Define and recognize apocalyptic writing.

Relate this genre to other Old Testament developments.

Relate this literature to later developments in eschatological thinking, including those in the New Testament.

14

God of History

One of the new theological discoveries that the people made as a result of the exile experience, was that YHWH is the God of all history. This discovery is related to the one about creation. If there is one God he must be the God of all creation; and all creation must give us new evidence about him. As we have seen, that was an exciting and productive theological seam. But also, if there is only one God, he must have designed not only the setting but also the story. That is, he must have designed history, and so history can also give us new evidence about him. The implications of this discovery are very wide-ranging. They include:

- The world has a purpose and destiny.
- History has a discernible design.
- Specific events within this history can be interpreted in relation to this design.
- Nothing happens by accident.
- The future is determined already – though only God knows its content.

To articulate and explore these discoveries a new 'ology' was formed, eschatology. And as one way of expressing eschatology, a new genre of writing appeared. It was resourced in part by the religious life of the Babylonians, and in part by a new sense of adventure with regard to the use of existing Old Testament images and symbols with which people would have been familiar. It was called apocalyptic, using a Greek word meaning 'revelation'. And what the writing in this style claimed to reveal is precisely what is outlined above. It claimed to reveal that which is known only to God, about history. In other words it claimed to have a revelation of the secrets of history: such things as when the earth would assume its final destiny, how exactly to interpret the signs of the times, and how to understand the design of history. It tried also to show how to develop an appropriate faith in response to this revelation, and how to understand God in a new way as a result of it. The Old Testament contains eschatological material in addition to that which is written in this particular genre. It could be said that the sum of this eschatological material is the final vision of the Old Testament about God and his relation with the world. Eschatology, as a whole, sets out the vision of what people hope for, who believe in a God who has control over history. As such it provides a substantial link with the New Testament both in terms of substance and of vocabulary. In this chapter we shall look first at the apocalyptic material, then at the wider picture.

Reflection on experience

Do you recognize the kind of quest set out above from your own experience, religious or secular? How central a place do you think it should have in religious life? What are the advantages and disadvantages of adopting this as the central plank of religious experience?

We look at the apocalyptic material first because it is the best defined and easiest to understand, even though it is among the latest material in the Old Testament. Other eschatological material is scattered in fragments throughout the Latter Prophets in particular, and is a little more difficult to organize, though after learning about apocalyptic it will be easier to make sense of. The book of Daniel is the most thoroughly apocalyptic book. Other fragments include: Ezekiel 38, 39; Isaiah 24—27; and Zechariah 9—14. Attempts to define apocalyptic normally work in two ways. First, it can be defined by its formal and literary characteristics; and second, it can be defined by its content.

Apocalyptic literature is just that – literature. It was written to be read, and is not the attempted recording of someone's speech. There is no real consensus as to the audience for this material but it certainly gained recognition at popular level, and its technical terms were familiar in New Testament times, at street level, and form the stuff of ordinary conversation. It looks a bit like ancient science fiction – and it does have some similarities with that more modern genre. For example it has a very strong moral tone and sees issues around good and evil in very black and white ways. It has three main literary characteristics.

- It is *esoteric*. That is, it deals in secrets which have only been revealed to certain privileged individuals. When you think that this literature claims to be opening up the secrets of history, hitherto known only to God himself, you can see why the author wants to invest the work with this kind of authority. The people who are credited with receiving this special knowledge are usually long-dead but revered and well-known figures from Israel's past story: people such as Noah or Isaac or even Adam. The idea is that secrets divulged to these important people have just come to light and can now be made public. The combination of secrecy and antiquity together with the name of an ancient worthy is what gives the work its authority.

- It is *pseudonymous*. Following from the above, the works are not written by the people whose names appear in the title. This was not the scandal in ancient times that it would be today. It was, in effect, an accepted device.

- It conveys its message with heavy dependence on *symbolism*. This too adds to the aura of secrecy. There is something to specially understand; a cipher to decode. The symbolism can be of many different kinds. Some of the symbols are universal, such as life and death or light and darkness. Some are symbols of cultural vitality used by others in Israel's traditional religious writing, such as the harlot or the serpent. Some have been borrowed from other cultures and are innovative, having been learned as a result of the Exile, such as stories about cosmic battles. Some of the symbols are animals, or fantastic combinations of human and animal features. Number symbolism is also important. People sometimes think of number symbolism as extremely crude, but actually it is a logical progression from a belief in the God of all creation. If God has really left his imprint in his creation then there ought to be clues in the perceived ordering of that creation as to significant numbers. So seven is obviously important, since there are seven days in a week. And four is also important, the number of weeks in a month; and there are four winds and four points of the compass. Being the number of months in a year, as well as the number of the 'tribes of Israel', 12 makes a link between nature and history. God's number is seven, the number of completeness. The number seven repeated emphatically three times, 777, is absolute completeness. That which claims to be God but which falls short could then be described as six. The absolute, and most extreme form of pretension to be God, would therefore be 666.

Hebrew letters of the alphabet, like Roman numerals, have a numeric value. This allows great creative scope for those who want to invest their apocalyptic work with lots of intriguing secrets just waiting to be discovered. The letter D, for example, has a value of 4, whereas the letter V has a value of 6. There are no vowels in Hebrew, so the word David (DVD) is worth 14. This is twice 7 (cue for excitement). This may look primitive, but it is how science begins and still, to an extent, operates, by trying to find laws of nature from a process of observation of the world. And this does have a huge popular appeal. One only has to recall how much attention is given to any ancient document, especially one in a strange language, that claims in some way to tell us what we do not already know about history and destiny, to take the point. Much of what is written about astrology appeals to the same kind of interest. We want to know what the future holds and are more impressed by the answers of those who have unlocked them from esoteric and fascinating inaccessible sources.

The 'plot' of apocalyptic usually involves: either describing a setting where the principal character sees fantastic visions and hears commentary on those visions; or describing some kind of journey (perhaps through the world of the dead, or through some of the seven heavens) where, again, fantastic things are seen and heard. However, fantastic though they seem, mysteriously enough, they usually have application to the very moment of history in which the reader stands. Therefore they have an immediacy that adds to their authority as well, so it's all pretty clever stuff.

The content of apocalyptic is to do with the agenda with which we began.

History has been predetermined and designed. It is therefore understood as being split up into different ages or epochs, each giving way to the next in some relatively cataclysmic way. It is key to understanding the genre that the reader is understood to be right at the end of an age, and on the cusp of the next age. Again this is a way of heightening immediacy. It's much more interesting to be alive in 1999, 2000 or 2001 than it is in, say, 1977. If there are to be (as there usually are) entry conditions of some kind for the next age, then the fact that the age is almost upon us means it is even more important to meet them. This gives the content an air of moral immediacy. The two things that are usually regarded as the main threats, in terms of human error, to entry into the new age, are immorality and idolatry. The fate of those who succumb to either of these is often recounted in graphic detail, as is the bliss of those who receive their reward for staying pure and faithful. The fact is that every action, however insignificant it seems, has cosmic significance.

Reflection on text

Read Daniel 7.1–14. This is a typical vision passage from the second half of the book of Daniel – the first half is a kind of 'novel' rather similar to the story of Joseph setting out how a wise man favoured by God conducts himself. This passage contains the most influential passage for New Testament eschatology from verses 13f. Read the whole passage to get the flavour of the genre. Identify, if you can, the typical elements we have outlined: fantastic imagery, fascination with the significance of numbers, the relation to current political events. What kind of people do you think might want or need to read something like this?

The way in which the new age is ushered in varies, but often involves God's human agent. This agent may be his anointed (Messiah) or, as the book of Daniel describes it, a son of man. There has been much discussion about the precise reference of this term, especially in Daniel 7.13, because the term Son of Man is the only one found on Jesus' lips in the Gospels to describe his own vocation. Ways of recognizing the signs that show the end is near usually correspond to historical occurrences at the time of writing. Within the new age, there will be a new justice. Everyone will get their just deserts at last, since evidently that does not happen here and now. This justice will be open even to those who have died. It is from this literature that a belief in resurrection of the dead derives. The first mention is at Daniel 12.2. This new dispensation where God's rule will be honoured in a new way can be described as the kingdom of God, another key New Testament term. The more that power to control and direct history is ascribed to God, the more distant he becomes. Hence, in apocalyptic writing, God is about as remote as we find him, while influencing, nevertheless, all that goes on in our lives. God's links to humankind are angels, and this literature sees the growth of angelology. To begin to understand this literature throws a whole new light on the New Testament Gospels and their concerns and mode of expression.

However, it is difficult to really understand what this literature is about without understanding the social context that gave birth to it. It has been described as a literature of the oppressed, and the assumption has been that it derives from a social context of suffering. The book of Daniel is dated to 163 BCE, and associated with the nationalist revolt against the imposition of Greek culture by the occupying power of the time. The genre as a whole flourished between this time and around 150 CE, a time of great political unrest punctuated with revolts. This was the kind of background that must have prompted wider questions about whether history had any purpose, and whether Israel had any vocation within it. It must have prompted more local questions as well about whether the sufferings and anxieties of the present were actually worth it, and whether individuals had either vocation or significance. Where was this God, who now seemed so far away, or was the whole thing just a cruel delusion? The cry of the psalmist 'How long?' in a sense sums it all up. But perhaps that still does not explain fully the rather bizarre nature of this material. Just what sort of real people could have written or wanted to read it, and what did it do for them?

I lived in a mining community during the British 1984 Miners' Strike, and that gave me more of an insight into the apocalyptic mindset than anything I had read. The situation had these characteristics.

- The community was depressed;

- They felt hemmed in on every side by a common enemy;
- The response to that common enemy produced what you might call a 'common faith';
- People were divided easily into friends and enemies, and all issues were black and white;
- Propaganda was a chief means of 'information';
- People felt vulnerable and powerless;
- There was a harking back to the old days, the days of Union heroes when such a thing could never have happened because the miners were too strong;
- There was a sense that this was a significant time. Whatever happened, things would never be quite the same again.

If we can imagine ourselves in such a community we are close to understanding the setting of apocalyptic. How did the writings, then, meet this situation?

- The writings gave the people confidence that this was indeed a significant time in history, and that history did have a meaning and purpose with God in control of it.
- It accepted that the readers felt like a powerless minority and provided visions of their being vindicated. Though it did not look like it, they were in fact right and they had in fact won.
- It heightened the moral stakes to provide a clearer definition of who was 'in' and who was 'out'.
- It gave a new sense of vocation to the people. In the new age they would have role and purpose.
- It assured people that there would be a new justice in the new age, and so, that their suffering was not in vain.

This was an extreme form of eschatological writing but in some degree the questions it addressed were, and remain, common for those who believe in a God of all history. They are questions about destiny and purpose and they are often prompted by contexts of suffering, or events which seem difficult to relate to the plans of a good and loving God, or events which seem so terrible that God's very existence is called into question because of them.

In addition to these kinds of question, there is the more optimistic faithful kind of hoping which sees what is wrong with the world and looks to a future in which God will put it right. Other eschatological fragments in the prophets speak to these wider questions and longings.

Gowan (2000) helpfully organizes the material under three headings, all of which he sees evidence for in Ezekiel 36—38. What it amounts to in his view is the perceived need for a threefold transformation. There is the *need to transform the human person* (36.25–7); the *need to transform human society* (36.24, 28, 33–6), and the *need to transform nature itself* (36.30, 35).

Reflection on text

Read Ezekiel 36. Can you see the three kinds of transformation described above? What do you think they involve? Check your response against the discussion which follows.

The transformation of the human person needs new forgiveness and a new sense of starting again – almost a new creation. It is interesting to note that the idea of forgiveness only becomes a key theological theme after the experience of exile. It is a key component of the D way of thinking that Israel was guilty and deserved to be punished. God's forgiveness is a new example of his graciousness. Though Israel had not deserved to be able to have a second chance to enter the land, any more than she had a right to enter the land in the first place, nevertheless God forgave her and so made possible something new (Isaiah 40.2). Both forgiveness and new creation become important New Testament theological ideas. Indeed it could be said that forgiveness is the hot new topic that Jesus himself makes central to his proclamation.

The transformation of human society looks to the past for models on which to base hopes for the future. The idealized version of David's kingdom exemplifies the new hopes for a society that is united, joyful, strong through justice, blessed by God in a special way and attended by his presence, peaceful and harmonious, even in a new international and ecumenical way. Victory over the nations will lead to peace with the nations, and finally to their conversion. From this model we find reference to the new kingdom of God, and to a new anointed one, 'Messiah', even a new son of God. This too takes theological debate forward. What will be the conditions for entry to this kingdom? What will its characteristics be? These are key issues addressed again in the New Testament Gospels, themselves building on the debate in inter-testamental literature.

The transformation of nature itself begins with a dissatisfaction about the natural order. This reflection, we must remember, is taking place in a part of the world beset by natural as well as man-made disasters, such as famine and earthquake. It is also a world which is far from safe because of wild animals, poisonous insects and the like. What is required is a new dispensation in which people can sit in safety and security under their vine and fig tree with none to hurt destroy or cause alarm (Micah 4.4); where the lion will lie down with the lamb and the child can play with snakes and all will be well (Isaiah 11.6–9). There will be a new fertility and abundance; the oil will be overflowing. The world will be safe. There will be a new heaven and a new earth.

Jerusalem comes to play a pivotal role in uniting these three strands of eschatological thinking. Herein lie the roots of Zion theology, which is ultimately successful to the extent that Isaiah is a text preferred by New Testament writers who want to locate Jesus theologically. The new Jerusalem is a theme in later New Testament writings, and the place of Jerusalem in the narrative of Jesus' death has much more 'edge' as a result.

The new reflections on what it means to think of YHWH as a God of history, then, lead to some of the most mature thinking in the Old Testament about God and the world, and to a definition of what religion is about, and what hopes it encapsulates and symbolizes, which is really quite modern and recognizably contemporary. On the one hand this thinking results from a new inspiration about the vocation of Israel and the future of religion. It results from a new theological possibility opened up by the experience of exile. But it also results, ironically, from disappointment and disillusion with the evidence of a present in which the vision seems far from realization, and in which faith is at odds with experience. Some would say that this is the usual context for all mature Christian belief nowadays. Despite its relative paucity in the Old Testament this material has great theological importance and helps build the new theological landscape after the Exile.

CHAPTER 15 SUMMARY

What is this chapter about?

This chapter deals with the book of Job and, in passing, Ecclesiastes. There is a full discussion of the content of the book and the issues it raises, both in its original context and for contemporary readers.

What books are referred to?

J. H. Eaton, *Job* (Sheffield: JSOT Press, 1987); Norman Whybray, *Job* (Sheffield: Sheffield Academic Press, 1998), John Holdsworth, *Dwelling in a Strange Land* (Norwich: Canterbury Press, 2003).

What other books would be helpful?

A very readable introduction is Ellen van Wolde, *Mr and Mrs Job,* trans. John Bowden (London: SCM Press, 1997). A well regarded additional series of commentaries is that by David Clines in the Word series, in three volumes (Waco, Texas: Word Books, 1989, 2000, 2005).

How is the chapter organized?

The chapter adopts the book's own structure and offers description, commentary and application suggestions.

What should I be able to do by the end of this chapter?

Describe the contents of the book of Job.

Recognize some of the current critical issues in relation to this work.

Relate this work to other Old Testament writings.

15

I'm a Righteous Man – Get Me Out of Here!

Anyone who has been involved in pastoral care, from a religious background of any kind, will know that probably the most difficult situations, and they are among the most frequent, are those that involve bad things happening to good people. People want to know why people do not get their just deserts. Why is it that people who do bad things do not always appear to have to face bad consequences, and why is it that people who do good things are not exempt from bad experiences? At one level this is a pastoral problem, but it points to a deeply theological problem about the nature of God. The book of Job is the Old Testament's most profound contribution to this area of the understanding of life.

Reflection on experience

Is this an area of life with which you are familiar – either as one who has experienced great grief, or one who has tried to minister to people in that situation? How did it go? Did God feature in the process at all? Based on your experience, what kinds of question would you want this book to illuminate for you?

It is part of the wisdom literature, but it displays the new intellectual religious freedom that this development calls for, in that it completely subverts the message of the book of Proverbs, and radically challenges the very foundations of religious belief as it had been exemplified thus far. It departs from much biblical writing in that it is overtly a work of fiction. Its opening lines more or less add up to 'once upon a time in a land far away'. But there is nothing infantile about the issues with which it deals. The opportunity this new genre gives for setting up a hypothetical situation that throws the issues into sharpest relief is exploited to the full. In modern times, the author would no doubt have been producer of a reality TV show with a title like: *I'm a Righteous Man – Get Me Out of Here!* From a literary critical point of view, this is particularly interesting. Throughout the book, the reader knows things that the characters do not know, and it is possible to speak openly about the author's strategy for managing the reader – the starting-point of rhetorical criticism. And yet the narrative sections of the book are very few, coming at the beginning to set the thing up, and right at the end. Interestingly, also, the end part of the narrative makes little reference to the beginning.

This is the setup. Job is a good and religious man, who does everything he should according to what one might call a pre-trauma or innocent view of religion and religious life. He makes the right sacrifices. He even makes sacrifices for sins that might have been committed. He is a model father. He is 'blameless and upright'. He is also wealthy, offering living proof of the view of the book of Proverbs that good living brings its rewards; and of the kind of sentiment we read in, for example, Psalm 37.25–40, that the righteous will not be forsaken and will have descendants, safety and power, in sharp contrast to the wicked. Job has land, family, cattle and presumably power. He was 'the greatest of all the people of the east' (Job 1.3). But then all this changes. We are transported as readers into the realm of the heavenly council where God is chatting to his Minister without Portfolio, Satan. God is portrayed as being very proud of Job and presenting him as a model: 'Have you considered my servant Job? You will find no-one like him on earth.' Satan is cynically unimpressed and retorts that Job has every reason to be pious because he's been so successful. Would his devotion be so strong if things started to go wrong? In the story, God is willing to put it to the test on the condition that Job is not harmed personally. So we return to earth to find that all Job's marks of success – his crops, possessions, even his family – have all been lost in a series of bizarre tragic events. But God is proved right in his wager with Satan. Job maintains faith: 'Naked I came from the womb, naked I shall return whence I came. The Lord gives and the Lord takes away; blessed be the name of the Lord' (Job 1.21).

Once again we, the reader, are privy to a conversation between God and Satan at the Council meeting. God makes his point: 'You incited me to ruin him without cause but he still holds fast to his integrity' (2.3). Satan's response is to say that the rules were skewed because God did not allow any personal harm to come to Job. 'Just reach out your hand and touch his bones and his flesh, and see if he will not curse you to your face' (2.5). God continues the wager with the stakes thus raised and allows Job to be afflicted with painful running sores. His one condition is that Job should not be killed. Still Job does not curse God. But in chapter 3 he curses just about everything else. By this point he has been joined by three other 'friends', and for the remainder of the book the main interest centres on the conversations between these three and Job. The wager is never again referred to. Satan is no longer a player.

Once, historical questions about the provenance of the story, its original location and date were considered important. Now the main questions for commentators concern:

- what the book is actually about: that is, what really is the question being addressed?
- how the book manages its rhetorical strategy; and
- the relation of the book to other wisdom literature, and to the canon of scripture generally.

Some commentators (e.g. Eaton 1987) believe the issue with which Job deals is the one stated, namely: Is there such a thing as disinterested piety? Does Job fear God for naught? (as Satan puts it). In fact Eaton wants to develop this further into the question: Is there such a thing as disinterested love, or does self-interest inevitably override altruism? Whybray (1998) believes the issue is to do with the nature of God and the human incapacity to understand him. Many others believe the problem to be that of theodicy – the problem of evil. If God is both good and powerful why is there evil in the world and why, in particular, does it afflict good people? Writers who take the Exile as the fundamental starting-point of Old Testament theology see

Job as a response to the kinds of theological crisis and development we have outlined in the previous two chapters.

Certainly it goes with the grain of recent work to see the post-exilic writings as connected with each other in some way. We have already seen how the new understanding of YHWH as God of all creation and God of all history leads to questions about justice, purpose and destiny. How could the kind of God in whom you'd want to believe, the liberator God of the traditions, have designed history in a way which leaves so much injustice? How could a good creator God have designed the world in a way that allows the innocent to suffer? In other words, questions about suffering or the nature of God are intimately connected to the new theological venturing which the Exile has demanded and allowed, and to that extent, all the proposals above are credible. Standing behind them however, surely, is the bigger question of what it means to be religious in a post-experience, post-trauma situation in which the old certainties no longer have currency. Viewed in this light the positions adopted by Job's first three friends represent ways of being religious that the author wants to challenge. It is as if someone who has suffered a terrible adult trauma, whose young bride has just committed suicide, let's say, is trying to make sense of everything using only resources available in a kindergarten Sunday school. The theological certainties that stand behind the book of Proverbs must fall into that category, and the book of Job says quite clearly that it just will not do. As we have said, it is possible to read the section of the book which deals with the friends' arguments from a purely pastoral point of view. They demonstrate clearly how not to do it, and they have many modern resonances as we shall see. But pastoral work can never be divorced from the theology that motivates, feeds and legitimizes it. The book of Job then is about God, justice, suffering and piety. But it is no disinterested academic discussion. The choice of the subject suggests that the outcome matters to the author, and that he really wants to know what it can mean, practically, to be a religious person in the new situation.

Chapters 3 to 27 present the problem through the speeches of four people. Job's three friends each speak in turn, and Job replies to each in a way that refuses to accept the position which that friend has promoted. The discussion is robust, conducted in a fairly stilted poetic way and only just falls short of caricature. The three friends are happy, it seems, to live their lives on religious bases which to Job have been discredited through experience. One of the ironies of the book is that although the initial pictures are of God and Satan having a bit of a flutter, and essentially making something of a game of Job's agony – a very uncomfortable picture for any follower then or now – that is the only picture of God available to those who hold the views of the friends.

After Job's initial cursing outburst in chapter 3, the first friend to speak is Eliphaz. This probably casts him as the eldest. Certainly he relies on his 'experience' (ironically enough, in a situation where faith and experience have been put at odds with each other) to deal with the situation pastorally. There are three points to his view. First is his appeal to experience, articulating the view of other wisdom writings, Psalms and right-wing newspapers, that everyone knows people get what they deserve. If people are poor it's their fault. If people suffer they must have done something wrong. He backs this view up with a self-authenticating vision. God has spoken to him in a very dramatic way in the night. Who could challenge such a thing? He concludes with what sounds like a well-worn set of clichés, culminating in the point: 'Do not despise the discipline of the Almighty' (5.17). What is being presented here is a view of life which sees God as operating under certain rules. Religious people understand these rules and live their lives accordingly. One of the axioms is that suffering is the result of sin. If bad things have happened there must be a reason. We can see how this view could result from one reading of creation theology. In the view of Eliphaz, what Job has to do is accept his guilt and confess it. There might have been a time when Job would have accepted this view. When he himself was successful and unaffected he even gave similar advice to others. But the post-experience Job rubbishes this view. He refuses to believe in such a mechanical form of religion that has an easy explanation and easy remedy for every situation.

The position of the second friend, Bildad, is not dissimilar but his argument is framed differently. He comes straight to the point and dismisses Job's response as 'the long-winded ramblings of an old man' (8.2). His appeal is to tradition. This is what people have always believed and it is arrogant to think we know better. The irony here is that the reader knows that everything has in fact changed and that these are exciting days for theology. New avenues are being opened. This is a time of new imperatives and new permissions.

Lying behind this is perhaps a question about the appropriate use of tradition, just at a time when the concept of a canon of scripture is beginning to emerge. Is this something that will fossilize religious life, or will the traditions offer a point of reference in some other way? Job's response to Bildad betrays another fear for post-experience would-be believers. That is, that the creator God who has set up all these rules by which the whole universe is governed, and who is too great to be challenged by anyone, might be too great to be interested in individual destinies. Job wants to believe that God still knows and cares about him personally. In fact it is interesting that the book of Job deals with issues which until now have been seen in corporate terms (the relationship between Israel and YHWH) in individual terms. The post-Exile God is portrayed as very distant in every new development. Only an incarnation, perhaps, could rescue the concept which is so important to Job, of personal relationship.

The third friend to speak is Zophar, who could be regarded as something of a modern theologian in the sense that he has the current theological jargon at his fingertips. He knows about wisdom. He is an expert. He sets out the principles on which Proverbs is based, but this cuts no ice with Job. At the end of this first cycle of speeches he accuses them, in a telling phrase (though, as a glimpse at a couple of alternative English translations will show, a difficult one to translate) of bringing their God in their hand (12.6). In other words, Job's accusation is that for all their grand words about the greatness of God, his friends have in fact restricted him to something understandable, definable and predictable; something that can be carried around and brought out when necessary. Creation theology demands more than this in understanding God, and the resolution of the book comes with great breathtaking statements about the greatness of God and the insignificance of humankind in comparison.

Reflection on text

Read Job 4, 5 (Eliphaz's first speech); chapter 8 (Bildad's first speech); and chapter 11 (Zophar's first speech). Do you recognize the points made above? Is any of these a model for good pastoral practice, do you think? Yet, can you sympathize with any of them? It might be useful to select one and try to frame the outline of his position in your own words.

Two more cycles of speeches then reiterate these basic positions. Chapter 28 stands alone as a meditation on God's wisdom. Job then resumes his final response to the friends. At the end of chapter 31 we read, 'Job's speeches are finished' (31.40). But then there is a new character, Elihu, whom most commentators regard as an intrusion into the text. He is an angry young man who reminds the readers what is at stake, but adds nothing new to the main conversation. Then God speaks from a whirlwind and describes his creation in his own words. This is reassuring to Job. The whirlwind may have symbolic significance. It may be that the reader is being asked to think of the anguish of Job as 'the whirlwind' and that God speaks to him not through religious systems and functionaries, but from within his own experience of pain. In any case, Job's short answer (42.1–6) is one which accepts God as God and sees being religious in a new way, outside systems, which has to do with trust in response to authenticity, and new assurance of the integrity of creation.

The narrative conclusion is largely unrelated to the introduction. Some find this disappointing in that it appears to describe a restitution in an 'all's well that ends well' kind of way. Job has new property and a new family. Others point out that having a new family is not an exact restitution. (Try telling someone who has just lost a child that, never mind, they're young enough to have another.) However, this may be reading too much into a portion of text whose main aim is to ratify the final position which the text outlines about religion and the religious life. The struggle in the main section of the book is not so much between God and Satan, or between Job and God, but rather between Job's view of God and that of his friends. And in that struggle Job's view is the one vindicated. That is the really subversive climax to the book. Throughout, the author has presented the tale in a way which suggests (s)he censures Job and encourages the reader to do likewise. Job is the blasphemer; the one who dares to argue with God and the accepted wisdom of the religious establishment. The friends are beyond criticism. They say what everyone says, safe in the haven of established practice. But it is Job who is vindicated and not them. The resolution is complete when Job abandons his self-absorption in the face of the true revelation of God, and ministers to his friends.

Reflection on text

Read Job 42. This chapter contains Job's final response and the narrative epilogue. How satisfying do you find this? Do you think that this does in fact say more than: 'all's well that ends well'? And if so, what? How well, for example, do you feel it has answered the questions you set out at the beginning of this chapter in the reflection on experience?

In a book which champions unresolvedness and possibility over against clear definition and religious systems, there is nevertheless a contribution to the problem of suffering which post-exilic theology unearthed. That is, that God can somehow be met in the whirlwind, that he shares suffering and understands it, and that experience does not have to be at odds with faith but that it can be part of God's revelation. We have seen the apocalyptic writers' response. For them the justice which is denied the righteous in this life will be accorded them in the next. The doctrine of resurrection (whose first mention is Daniel 12.2) is developed to put flesh on this. The other great post-exilic contribution to the issue is that of the servant songs in 2 Isaiah, raising the possibility of redemptive suffering: that good can be brought about through suffering.

The pastoral theological message of the book I have summarized elsewhere as follows.

The book affirms that robust debate with God and forthright anger directed towards God are both legitimate forms of religious discourse. The question as to what role ministry has in enabling, refereeing or interpreting this discourse might also be one we note. From the pastoral perspective, the book highlights especially the importance of paying attention to all aspects of need and not approaching profound human problems with ready made off the peg answers. People have to be heard where they are and as they are, and in the terms they choose. Refusal to allow this is as often as not tied up with the fears of the pastor at losing control, rather than with attempts to help minister effectively. The immutability of God, this God who is creator and designer of the world, its history and its peoples and who can choose to redeem, is finally seen as a theological axiom which can inspire and guarantee: which can lead to awe and not just fear. As creator, God is not only interested in punishment. As one who holds destinies in his hands he is interested in the fulfilling of destinies and the realising of creative possibility. (Holdsworth 2003, p. 59)

The book of **Ecclesiastes** is usually dated later than Job, and its message is a more developed subversion of the conventional wisdom view of things as presented in Proverbs. The book is a series of reflections on life, presented by an old man, perhaps speaking to a younger. Unlike Proverbs, which in the same context sets out the rules with a degree of certainty about the system which supports them, the author of Ecclesiastes finds no comforting metanarrative. The ways of God are not clear. Rational observation fails to discern meaning. In fact (in a favourite phrase) all is vanity and illusion. The book is not atheistic, but begins, like Job, from a realistic experience of life which seems to demonstrate that life had better be lived for the moment. Nothing in life is neat, and nothing about death is certain.

Reflection on text

Read Ecclesiastes 3. This is probably the best known chapter, though perhaps a little untypically upbeat. How attractive do you find this view of life? Can you discern elements of theology here from either Proverbs or Job?

I recall teaching these books to a class of potential ministers. I asked them to sum up in a phrase if they could what was the experience to which these books spoke. I can do no better than reproduce the effort of one intelligent quite evangelical student who I think surprised himself as he said: 'Shit happens.'

CHAPTER 16 SUMMARY

What is this chapter about?

This chapter looks at the book of Psalms. It outlines reading strategies, and sketches critical approaches from the immediate past, together with some contemporary views and approaches.

What books are referred to?

The following new books are referred to: Michael Goulder, *The Psalms of the Return, Book 5, Pss 107–150* (Sheffield: Sheffield Academic Press, 1998); J. D. Pleins, *The Psalms: Songs of Tragedy, Hope, and Justice* (Maryknoll, NY: Orbis Books, 1993); W. Brueggemann, *The Message of the Psalms: A Theological Commentary* (Minneapolis: Augsburg, 1984); Gerald H. Wilson, *The Editing of the Hebrew Psalter* (Chico, Calif.: Scholars Press, 1985); Patrick D. Miller, *Israelite Religion and Biblical Theology: Collected Essays* (Sheffield: Sheffield Academic Press, 2000).

What other books would be helpful?

The Psalms sections in, for example, Baker and Arnold (1999), Brueggemann (2003), Perdue (2001) and Barton (1998) will all be useful. Works of classic scholars such as Gunkel and Mowinckel, referred to in the chapter, are best accessed in the first instance through these summaries.

How is the chapter organized?

The chapter follows these topics: how to read the book; form criticism and the Psalms, modern approaches to the book; Brueggemann's analysis; other contributions.

What should I be able to do by the end of this chapter?

Distinguish different reading strategies for the Psalms.

Outline the contribution of form critical method.

Understand current developments in scholarship and their implications.

16

Israel: The Musical

The accepted wisdom of the twentieth century is that the book of Psalms is a hymn book. Consequently people have tended to view the book in much the same way as a modern congregation might view its own hymn book: as secondary to other documents of faith. People do not generally think of their hymn books as a literary whole. They think of them as a collection, perhaps a fairly arbitrary collection, of individual items, which seem to invite the reader to look at those pieces as individual. It's sometimes interesting to know who wrote a particular hymn and in what circumstances. There will be lots of hymns that we never sing and have little interest in, but that doesn't matter. If we study a hymn book we shall pick out the items we like the best, and perhaps marvel at their poetry or the way they develop their theme, and that may help us in our individual devotions, but that's about it. If hymns are composed for particular kinds of liturgical occasion, and we happen to be interested in liturgy and the history of liturgy, that may give us another handle for study, but it's all pretty esoteric and something best left to those who have an interest in that kind of thing. In any case they're not as important as the Bible itself. That more or less sums up the twentieth-century approach to the Psalms as well, even though they're in the Bible.

Reflection on experience

If you have had contact with a faith community which uses a hymn book, does this describe your response? What other responses are possible, do you think?

In fact, such an approach does little justice even to modern hymn books. Collections of hymns are far from haphazard, and it is indeed interesting to see what editorial principles have dictated the organization of any one such book. Hymns are an extremely valuable resource, in particular, to the practical theologian, since they are concrete examples of a conversation between tradition and experience. They do open windows on to the theological understandings of the communities that use them. The kinds of questions that open those windows are for example:

- How closely related are the hymns to particular kinds of worship occasion? The hymnals of churches for which the eucharist is the primary act of worship, for example, tend to organize the book's contents around the actions and themes of that service. Those for whom more general expressions of praise are important organize their contents differently.
- Does the language of the hymns include technical or favoured terms, which suggest a particular editorial theological understanding? Are the hymns mostly about the church, or about Jesus or about the Spirit? In other words what are the editorial theological preferences?
- Do the hymns have a common idiom? If so, is it an open and exploratory, suggestive one, suitable for those searching after faith and meaning; or are the hymns capable of being sung only by those who are fully signed up to a particular understanding of faith?
- What kind of balance is there between religious and secular language in the hymns? Does that suggest an editorial preference in the question about the proper relationship between the church and the world?
- What popular hymns have not been included and why?
- Is there an obvious ecumenical dimension to the collection?

And so on.

Reflection on experience

Try to get hold of any hymn book from any tradition and interrogate it using the questions above and any others you can think of. What have you learned about this book as a result of this enquiry? Is it important to know what you have discovered, do you think?

All of these questions enable us to get closer to the way in which theology, and particularly the role of the worshipping community, is understood by the editor of the collection, and to some extent, perhaps, by those who use it.

Throughout most of the twentieth century, however, questions which assume an editorial hand, and want to make that the handle of interpretation, have rarely been asked. Rather, the book of Psalms has been used by historical critical scholars to gain a better understanding of 'what really happened in worship', with all the assumptions that implies. At the literary level there has been interest in the form and metre of the poetry and the provenance of the images used. Alongside that, individual psalms have continued to be read and studied from a devotional perspective. From the late twentieth century to the present there has been a discernible shift. Now there is much more interest in the book as a whole, and a tendency to take seriously its own division into five parts. There is a stronger assumption of editorial activity and a consequential shift in the kinds of theological information the book is expected to produce. The general move towards diversity of readings, and away from the assumption that there is one correct reading which expertise can reveal, is evidenced in recent work on the Psalms. There is an attempt to read the Psalms in a way that reveals their contemporary significance and which goes beyond the former individual devotional readings. As scholars have taken the finished work as a whole more seriously, there is less talk of this being a collection of hymns, and more of its being some kind of diverse statement about the history and experience of Israel. Perhaps it would not be overstating the case to describe the book from this perspective as *Israel: The Musical*.

But that is not how it began. The father of modern critical study of Psalms is Herman Gunkel, who is one of the great pioneers of form criticism. This method is particularly important to students of history as it offers a way both of tracing the development, the pre-history, of texts, and of organizing those texts. Psalms was an obvious example of a text to which the method could be applied. The context in which Gunkel worked was one which assumed:

- No editorial hand.
- A late date for the collection and perhaps for the majority of the psalms themselves. This was perceived as the hymn book of the second temple.

It was commonplace for commentators to regard psalms such as 137, which clearly derive from an Exile context, as among the earliest.

- That the Psalms were primarily for private devotion. The personal emphasis was evidence of a late date.
- The situations of conflict described fitted a second-century context.
- References to YHWH's anointed were in fact references to the Maccabean princes.

Gunkel established that the context in real life, the *Sitz im Leben*, of the Psalms was in fact public worship. So, a solution was found to the problem of sudden changes of psychology in the middle of Psalms such as at 22.22; 54.4; 55.22; 91.14–16 and 122.1f. These were not sudden mood changes in an individual. The sudden changes were to be understood as movements in liturgy. Psalms were in fact public, official and anonymous. Gunkel also argued that many of the psalms were much earlier in date than had previously been believed. This was especially true, he thought, of psalms which were about Jerusalem such as 46 and 48. As a result of this new thinking the Psalms came to be seen as a resource for knowledge about the religious life of Israel, the so-called cultus. Further attempts to locate the historical context of individual psalms have not generally been regarded as successful. The most recent attempt is that of Goulder (1998). Only Psalm 137 can be placed unequivocally from internal evidence. Gunkel's work became the launching-pad for others to work in the area of cultus research. Prominent among them was Sigmund Mowinckel, who became particularly interested in the references in the Psalms to YHWH as king, and who developed the thesis that an annual enthronement festival was the defining religious worship of ancient Israel. Other work concentrated on the relationship between what it was assumed Psalms bore witness to, and other manifestations of religious life such as prophecy or wisdom – all still in the context of attempting some form of historical reconstruction or narrative.

The form-critical method demanded first of all that the Psalms be classified according to genre or *Gattung*. The assumption behind this work was that we had been left a hymn book without an index, contents or an organizing principle. Nowadays, some hymn books simply list hymns alphabetically without reference to their subject. Until recently it was more common to list hymns under such headings as 'Praise and Thanksgiving', 'For use at a Baptism', or 'Missionary Hymns'. The work for which Gunkel is best remembered, and whose results are still used, is this work of classification. The *Hymn* was just one form he discovered, and he saw variations in its use. Songs of Zion (e.g. 48, 84), *Royal Psalms* (e.g. 2, 20—21 and 45) were related to particular occasions in the life of the king, such as battle, accession, or marriage. Some psalms were liturgies (such as 24, 68, 132) and some were wisdom psalms (e.g. 1). *Thanksgivings*, both individual (such as 145) and communal (such as 118) were another category. But by far the most interesting and numerous were the Psalms which could be called *Communal Laments* (such as 44) and *Individual Laments* (such as 22 and 38). This last category is the most numerous of all, and has occasioned further detailed work, most notably by Westermann.

Reflection on text

Read Psalm 22. This is one of the best known laments in the Psalter, since it is quoted in the New Testament on the lips of Jesus himself. See if you can discern the structure which Westermann finds in the laments. There is a twofold structure consisting of plea and praise. The plea has: an address to God; a complaint; a petition that God will act; a recital of reasons why God might (or even should) act; and an imprecation that satisfaction will not come until vengeance has been meted out. The praise element contains: an assurance of being heard; a declaration of the speaker's good faith; and doxology and praise.

There appears to be some kind of classification system built into the book of Psalms, through the superscriptions which appear with many of them. (These count as an extra verse in Hebrew, so the verse numbers in Hebrew and English Bibles are slightly different.) These superscriptions give us information about the type of composition. Psalms 120—134, for example, are called Songs of Ascents and may have been used by pilgrims going up to Jerusalem for some special liturgical occasion. Other descriptions appear more technical and their significance is not always clear. Further information

includes references to authors, or perhaps to the tradition which has created the psalm. David and Asaph are mentioned regularly. The critical consensus is that ascriptions of authorship are not to be read literally, but rather
as referring to a tradition, or a later interpretative guide. So for example
Psalm 51, which is traditionally ascribed to David's crisis period after the
Bathsheba episode. Sometimes there is a reference to a specific occasion of
use. So Psalm 30, for example, is for use on the occasion of the dedication
of the temple, while 92 is for the sabbath day. Technical musical expressions are sometimes used. 'To the choirmaster' is used 55 times. Psalm 45,
a marriage song, contains the strange instruction 'according to lilies' alongside other information that this is a love song, that it is for the Korahites and
that it is a maskil. It may be that this describes the tune, or it may be that
lilies featured in the marriage ceremony as a symbol of fertility, and that the
song was to be sung at that point. Yet other psalms point towards specific
historical circumstances (e.g. 52: 'When Doeg the Edomite came and told
Saul that David had gone to Abimelech's house'). These may well be later
additions, but what they add to the psalm or why it was thought useful to
include them is unclear.

A re-examination of what was once disregarded is now part of the 'letting
the text speak for itself' which characterizes more modern approaches with
their variety of readings. This also includes taking more seriously the division of the book of Psalms into five books each with its own doxology (as at
the end of Psalms 41, 72, 89, 106 and 150, though in fact the last few psalms
may be a doxology to the whole collection). Feminist readings have suggested, for example, that Psalms 6 and 55 are the laments of a woman who
has been raped. Works such as J. D. Pleins, *The Psalms: Songs of Tragedy,
Hope, and Justice* (1993), read the Psalms from a liberationist perspective.
Among other attempts to read the Psalms from a modern context is that
which Walter Brueggemann set out in his *Message of the Psalms*.

Brueggemann overlays the classification of Gunkel with a threefold classification of his own, which one might call a psychological or sociological
reading. His three categories are: Psalms of orientation, Psalms of disorientation and Psalms of re-orientation. The first category are those psalms which
speak of happy settledness and in which God is trustworthy, transparent
and reliable. Psalm 33 would be one example. In these psalms God is in his

heaven and all is right with the world. They exemplify a simple creation faith. Life is a protected space without anxiety. Those who use these psalms are the 'upright' or the 'righteous' who accept the creation/wisdom view of the good life, and feel that life is treating them well because they're doing the right things. For these people faith has little cost and many benefits. These are pre-trauma feelings. There is a focus on 'us' and the way in which we trust. Though some of the psalms in this category are among the best loved they are problematic. This kind of theology is normally favoured by the well off and those who have not had to question the easy link between good living and good fortune. There is a sense of denial about the experience of painful living which is the lot of many. This faith is exclusive. It may be that these psalms and this expression of faith is OK for children, who need to have a view of the world in which things are certain and relationships trustworthy: in which life is secure and the rules and boundaries are clear. The problem comes when adults sing these songs without the degree of self-awareness which can reinterpret them.

Reflection on text

Read Psalm 33. Do you see the scandal which Brueggemann sees?

Songs of disorientation include the laments which are so plentiful. These are post-trauma expressions of pain and grief. Psalm 74 would be one example. Brueggemann builds on the analytical work done by Westermann to show how grief is properly articulated in the community of faith. Songs of new orientation such as Psalm 30 describe the joy of surprise that there is life beyond death, hope beyond despair and new possibility in place of inevitable pain. These are psalms in which words like 'deliverance', 'rescue', 'liberation' find meaning in real human experience. In this threefold process Brueggemann sets out the cycle of faith, something like a pastoral cycle, with which many modern readers will be able to identify. Maturity in faith means moving from the easy assumptions of childhood faith through the trauma of adult experience to a faith refashioned in new terms.

Brueggemann was also responsible for an early attempt to describe Psalms as a book: that is, to attempt to chart its structure and movements in the way one would describe any other book of the Bible. What he found was a book which was introduced by Psalm 1 with a message of simple obedience, and which had as a conclusion Psalm 150 with its message of undiluted praise. In between is a treatment of the experiences of life in which Psalm 73 is a critical turning-point as it describes both suffering and hope. Such authentic insights into the struggles and setbacks of life give depth to the final summons to praise (Brueggemann 1991). Other writers have observed that since the Psalter opens with a summons to meditate on the Torah, this is tantamount to declaring that the book of Psalms itself is now to be regarded as Torah. The fivefold division may be further evidence of that intention. Writers such as Westermann and Childs have pondered the distribution of royal psalms and sought significance in that. Most of these psalms occur in Books 1–3, for example. Thereafter, the emphasis is on YHWH's kingship.

Gerald H. Wilson's *The Editing of the Hebrew Psalter* (1985) is regarded by many as a landmark essay. As a student of Brevard Childs he was interested both in the final form of the text, and in the canonical arrangement of the book. One interesting feature of his work is his comparison between the Psalter and other hymnic collections from the ancient world, such as the Sumerian Temple Hymn collection or the Qumran Psalter, each of which, he demonstrates, has an editorial policy. With regard to the biblical Psalter he finds both explicit indicators as to an editorial hand such as the superscriptions, as well as tacit indicators, for which groups of psalms provide some evidence. For instance, in addition to the examples cited above, a number of psalms close with the word 'Hallelujah'. Sometimes the two kinds of evidence coincide. Psalms 120—134 are all titled 'A Song of Ascents', suggesting a liturgical usage certainly, and perhaps as specific a context as pilgrimage to Jerusalem.

Reflection on text

Read Psalm 122. This is one of the best known Songs of Ascent. Try to picture yourself as a pilgrim to Jerusalem using this psalm. What might you be doing in its various sections? Can you imagine the psalm being used for liturgical purposes?

These psalms occur in groups, and there is later evidence that this is based on liturgical usage. The psalms in question are 104—106, 111—117, 135 and 146—150. Wilson identifies these as coming at the ends of sections of the psalms (Wilson 1985, pp. 182–97). A further example is Patrick D. Miller's work on Psalms 15—24. He attempts to show a definite arrangement in these psalms of the kind that is called chiastic. That is, the nine psalms follow the pattern: ABCD, E, DCBA. The significance of this for him is that Psalm 19 is a Torah Psalm. This kind of study is of course open to the accusation that patterns are being discerned that were not intended. In itself that is not a problem for the literary critic, for whom the reader's perception has precedence over writer's intention in any case; but it does seem likely that the explicit indications are accompanied by the kind of implied editorial hand that Wilson and others have discerned.

The book of Psalms has come in from the critical cold. It is now studied as other books of the Old Testament, studied in relation to its canonical shape, and studied as a source of information about theological trends as well as cultic practice. In those terms it provides some information about, particularly, theological themes such as Jerusalem, Torah and Creation. There is a new drive to relate the Psalms to recognizable contemporary experience. Underpinning the critical quest is Gunkel's insistence that genre identification is the key to understanding the book and its organization. Canonical criticism has also legitimized Christian attempts to read a Christological message into the Psalms. New questions have been prompted by contemporary experience in congregations that use hymn books. How ecumenical is this collection? What editorial principles have been adopted in the collection? *Israel: The Musical* is set for a long run.

CHAPTER 17 SUMMARY

What is this chapter about?

This chapter contains description and discussion of the books of 1 and 2 Chronicles, Ezra and Nehemiah

What books are referred to?

No new books are referred to in this chapter.

What other books would be helpful?

The introductions mentioned thus far have helpful summaries, though you will find scholars much more willing to discuss the D histories than the books under scrutiny here (see for example Barton 1998, pp. 198–210). An exception is Ralph W. Klein's contribution to Perdue (2001), which is extremely clear and helpful in its own right, and points to other bibliography. A reliable commentary by a prolific author in this field is H. G. M. Williamson, *1 and 2 Chronicles* (Grand Rapids: Eerdmans, 1982).

How is the chapter organized?

The main topics for the chapter are: the order of the books in Hebrew and Christian Bibles; an account of the contents of 1 and 2 Chronicles; Ezra, Nehemiah; conclusion.

What should I be able to do by the end of this chapter?

Distinguish between the different historical writers of the Old Testament.

Judge historical accounts from a theological perspective.

Relate these texts to other Old Testament material.

17

Those Were the Days!

In Christian Bibles, the books of **Chronicles** are to be found in what looks like a 'history section' of the canon, immediately after 1 and 2 Kings and before Ezra and Nehemiah. This is extremely confusing for a number of reasons.

- Arguably, in the Old Testament as we have already seen with the Deuteronomistic History, so-called, the term 'history' means a presentation of a particular theological viewpoint through the medium of an historical narrative.
- The books of Chronicles were written considerably later than the D history, from a different perspective, and as a response to completely different questions in a different theological context, although they do draw on the D histories as a source.
- The juxtaposition of Chronicles and Ezra–Nehemiah has helped give credence to the view that these were the work of one hand. Ezra appears to pick up the narrative exactly from where Chronicles leaves it. It is also argued that there are similarities of style, vocabulary and content. However, the majority of scholars today do not hold that view.
- In the Hebrew canon, Chronicles (which is just one book there) is not followed by anything. It is the last book in the canon; a fact which some commentators believe merits more serious consideration than it has been wont to receive.
- The title of the book in the Hebrew canon is usually translated as 'The events of the days'. Given its theological purpose it might not be too fanciful to translate a little idiomatically 'Those were the days!'

The work is normally dated in the fourth century BCE, during the Persian period. It is part of the late post-Exile reflection on the vocation and purpose of Israel. It deals, as do the P writings, with which there are sympathies, with questions about the identity of Israel, but does so against the backdrop of the long communal memory of God's dealings with Israel thus far. The D histories in the books of Samuel and Kings had covered this ground to answer the question, 'How could God let the Exile happen?' They had answered the question in terms of the people's guilt, and particularly the fact that they were badly led by poor or weak kings. And so no weakness was left unpublicized in their attempt to make the argument. Even, or perhaps especially, King David's private life was subject to the kind of scrutiny so disliked by modern politicians. The Chronicler's question, on the other hand, is along the lines of: How can Israel understand its vocation and destiny in the context where it now finds itself, as a small Persian colony (Yehud), centred around a Jerusalem that was only rebuilt as the result of an act of great generosity by a Persian king? (It is worth comparing this question with those that the P writers addressed.) The Chronicler believes that a continuity needs to be demonstrated between pre-Exile Israel and the present context, and he does that through the institution of kingship and through the institutions of liturgical worship. So for him, Kings David and Solomon are key figures, the dignity of whose office at least needs to be maintained. Hence there is no 'kiss and tell' section in the book, and the whole tone is rather less tabloid and rather more serious. The Chronicler also reserves a definite place for the Levites, as those who have a key role in worship, and perhaps in the future formation of community theology, as we hear some of their temple sermons.

Reflection on text

Read 2 Samuel 11. This is the beginning of the so-called succession narrative or court history, and it deals in embarrassing detail with David's misdemeanours. Now read how the Chronicler deals with the same part of the story in 1 Chronicles 20.1–3. What is lost here? How strongly do you feel the different agendas? If we only had one of these accounts would it matter?

The two books, as they are printed in Christian Bibles, divide into easily recognizable sections. In reading them it is interesting to compare this presentation with that of the D histories, which they appear to follow. In doing so, of course, we must remember that both of these are interpretations. 1 Chronicles 1—9 is completely taken up with a genealogy (compare the strategy of the P writers). This genealogy is different from those in the P writings in that they are not a means of connecting two pieces of narrative. Rather they set out the grand design of the whole work, in the same kind of way that the geneaologies in Matthew (1.1–17) or Luke (3.21–38) operate in the New Testament. The most obvious theological point here is that the whole project begins with Adam (as does Luke's). This is to be a story with universal overtones. It is not just a story about a local god and some remote tribes. It is a story about humankind and the destiny of the world. In other words it reflects the monotheism, and the further reflections on God and history for which we have seen the evidence in other post-exilic writings. But as with Matthew's genealogy of Jesus, there is special interest in the family of David, marking him out as a special player in this drama. Also one whole chapter (chapter 6) is given over to a history of the Levites, making special reference to their service in the house of God; and to the role of Aaron and his descendants as priests (6.49ff.).

Chapter 10 deals briefly with Saul, but only in order to introduce David and contrast him favourably with Saul. Then follows the major portion of 1 Chronicles, describing the reign of David (chapters 11—29). The account is recognizable from that in the D history, though quite different from it. There is no lengthy struggle with Saul. David assumes the throne as one born and called to it, without great trauma. There is no account of David's dysfunctional family with their incestuous relationships and murder, as we find in the D account. Here David is principally the unchallenged and relatively untroubled ruler. The high point in this account is the promise made to David and his family, for ever, in chapter 17, which sets out the new theological perspective most clearly. Five chapters are devoted to the plans to build the temple (22—26), with special attention to the roles of the priests and the Levites (chapter 23). David is thus presented as having masterminded the design of the temple and its life, though it is left to Solomon to build it. The continuity between the two is established in chapter 29, which includes one of the few passages within these books familiar to Christian readers.

Reflection on text

Read 2 Chronicles 2. This chapter describes Solomon's building plans. Reading the chapter carefully: do you discern any touches of irony here? Look, for example, at the use of the phrase, 'and a royal palace for himself'. You might like to refer again to 1 Samuel 8.10–18, with its warnings about how kings operate.

---

2 Chronicles 1—9 then picks up the story of Solomon building the temple, an account which culminates in the visit of the Queen of Sheba, an opportunity to outline the lavish splendour of Solomon's lifestyle. The remainder of 2 Chronicles continues the history of the kings of Judah until the Exile, maintaining the D emphasis on the culpability of the people of Judah and their kings in the eventual tragedy. The final verses of the book take the narrative beyond the point where it ends in 2 Kings 25.30, to the point where the exiles are to be allowed to return home. The way in which this is framed is interesting. Cyrus, the conquering king of Persia, is presented in a very positive way (compare Isaiah 45.1, where as we have seen he is described as Messiah). The writer says that the Lord inspired him to issue his decree, and the words of the decree itself show Cyrus giving great respect to 'The Lord, the God of heaven', who has given Cyrus 'all the kingdoms of the earth' and who has, according to the decree, charged Cyrus with building a temple in Jerusalem. In every respect this presentation casts Cyrus as the agent of God's will. The final words of the decree, 'Whoever among you belongs to his people, may the Lord his God be with him, and let him go up', are the final words of the Hebrew Bible, and as such offer a defiantly optimistic model for Jews living in occupation, or as sojourners in foreign lands. They also emphasize the new universal message of the faith, and point to the issue of identity (who is to count as one of God's people?) which is set to become one of the great religious arguments of succeeding generations. They also have a striking 'reality' about them as the words of those who, with great

self-awareness, know themselves to be at the mercy of this foreign king, who nevertheless can exhibit some of the characteristics of a Lord's Messiah.

In the course of this account we hear little or nothing of the history of the north. The true Israel is the one perpetuated in Judah, and this is recognizably in descent from David. The northern leaders are portrayed as recalcitrant (2 Chronicles 10.19; 13.4–12). The emphasis on the south means there is no narrative around the exploits of Elijah and Elisha and sparse mention of northern kings. The Chronicler does consider prophets as important players in the drama, regarding them especially as people who rebuke error and keep kings in line. However, political division does not annul the religious unity of Israel. Israel is an inclusive concept. It is interesting that in the Chronicles Jacob is always called Israel, for instance. There is a sense in these books that although the lineage of David is important, there is something far more universal that stands behind it – namely the kingship of God (1 Chronicles 28.5; 29.23). It is interesting to compare 2 Samuel 7.16 with 1 Chronicles 17.14. In the former David is told: '*your* kingdom will be established for ever in my sight'. In the latter he is told rather, 'I will give him a sure place in *my* house and *my* kingdom.' This hope that the kingdom is, in the final analysis, in God's hands, accords with post-exilic expressions of hope (e.g. Daniel 7.14) and finds expression at, for example, 2 Chronicles 20.6: '. . . are you not the God who is in heaven? You rule over all the kingdoms of the nations; in your hand are strength and power, and there is none who can withstand you.'

The temple is clearly an important symbol of continuity and identity for this community. The Chronicler links the king to the temple, joining the two establishment institutions of Israel in a way that makes the Sinai covenant with its 'bottom-up' people-based injunctions hugely inferior to a top-down model in which God acts through institutional agents. The writer sees the temple tradition in a positive and even dynamic way. He is not just an arid preserver of ritual, any more than were the P writers, and he is as open to people enjoying themselves as the next person (1 Chronicles 12.38–40), but specifically in connection with worship. In Levitical sermons faith in God is stressed rather than ritual observance, and links made with the prophets (2 Chronicles 20.14–17; 29.25). Also, the temple is not indispensable. Piety is possible in other contexts. Soldiers at war can simply turn toward Jerusalem wherever they are and their prayer will be heard (2 Chronicles 6.34). Even those who are ritually unclean can still participate (2 Chronicles 30.18–20).

For this writer, though, experience has taught a certain black-and-whiteness in analysing experience. Faithfulness leads to blessing and success. Those who forsake God fall prey to disease, defeat and despair (1 Chronicles 10.13–14; 28.9); the Chronicler's most popular words are 'forsake', 'seek', and 'unfaithfulness'. The books of Ezra and Nehemiah give us more context in which to consider his work. With these two books, the story of the formation of Judaism is, in effect complete. Ezra and Nehemiah are two complementary leaders. Nehemiah, acting at the prompting of the Persian authority, sets himself the task of rebuilding the temple in ravished Jerusalem, and his book tells the story of how that was achieved. Ezra's task of reconstruction is more ideological. He is the person who oversees the re-branding of the Jewish community as the people of the book – the book in question being the Torah.

The book of **Ezra** is dated around 458 BCE, and picks up the story where Chronicles had left it, with the decree which allows the Jews to return to Jerusalem, and Cyrus's invitation to rebuild the temple. The first six chapters describe the return and the early years of the pioneers, culminating in the temple's being built and the Passover festival being celebrated there. In this section some cross-reference is possible with the writings ascribed to the 'prophets of the Return' Zechariah and Haggai, who are mentioned by name in the text. Chapters 7—10 concentrate more on Ezra himself. His credentials are spelled out at Ezra 7.6: 'He was a scribe, expert in the law of Moses which the Lord the God of Israel had given them. The king granted him everything he requested, for the favour of the Lord his God was with him.' In these short sentences Ezra is set up as the king's man and God's man, as well as being, in a sense, Moses' successor. From the outset there is tension between the returnees and those who have remained in the land throughout the period of exile. Remarkably, it is the former who are to be taken as the yardstick of genuineness rather than the latter. In Ezra 4.3 we read that only the returnees are to be allowed to participate in the rebuilding of the temple, despite offers of help from elsewhere. Chapter 9, though, is the strongest statement of what will be a decisive theme of the book: the maintenance of racial purity as a means of establishing religious identity.

Reflection on text

Read Ezra 9. How much of a scandal does this seem to you now? Can you have any sympathy with the concerns that give rise to this kind of religious organization? You might like to reread Isaiah 56 to see an alternative view.

Chapter 9 deals with the problem of mixed marriages. The news that 'the holy race' (literally 'seed') has become mixed with the alien population fills Ezra with dismay (9.4). In a prayer which acts as a summary of his argument (9.6–15) he defines purity in terms of race or seed, making mixed marriages acts of defilement, and so he declares that all such mixed marriages must be dissolved. Here we see a philosophy which will lead inevitably to a particular view of identity, as the Jewish community continues to be an occupied minority at home, and with the larger part of their number part of the Dispersion or Diaspora in a variety of other countries. Although the books of Ezra and Nehemiah describe the events of the Return in a way that gives one possible understanding of Jewish identity, the vast majority of the descendants of the original deportees to Babylon did not return. It was a small minority, who reacted to the threat of their extinction by setting stringent controls on social life to maintain purity, which accomplished this definition of who was really Jewish and who was not. Questions about 'who really belongs' are common among 'peoples' who do not have a land, or sovereignty in their land. The same kind of questions are raised in communities of Palestinians and Kurds today, as well as Jews.

The book of **Nehemiah** (444 BCE) contains similar themes. Scholars accept the historicity of both books, in the sense that they provide reliable accounts of the events they do describe. However, the material included is very selective, there are huge gaps, and it is accepted that the production of a reliable historical text is not the authors' prime intention. For example, the simple phrase, 'after these things', at Ezra 7.1 can cover a gap of some fifty years. Much of Nehemiah is written as a first-person account (for example chapters 1—2, 4—6, and parts of chapters 7, 12 and 13), and there has been some interest in whether the book may be a redaction of a 'memoir of Nehemiah'. This would not necessarily mean that the authorship could be traced to Nehemiah himself. It could equally well have been the product of a group of admirers. Certainly the account casts him in a very favourable light, primarily as a gifted administrator who gets things done. The climax of the book will be the reaffirmation of the Covenant (9.38—10.39), but the text outlines the process which leads to that point.

The first six chapters outline Nehemiah's position in the Persian court and his commission to return to Jerusalem to oversee the rebuilding of the ruined city. Chapter 5 is particularly interesting, especially in the light of the larger purpose to establish a Torah-based community. In this chapter Nehemiah outlines reforms in the field of social justice. He declares that present practices with regard to servicing debt in particular are downright wrong, in terms reminiscent of eighth-century prophets. He exacts a promise that from now on things will be organized according to what are regarded as true Torah-like principles. He involves the priests in an oath-taking ceremony to set the promises in a religious context, and finally he engages in something very much like a prophetic act, in that: 'I shook out the fold of my robe and said, "So may God shake out from house and property every man who fails to keep this promise. May he be shaken out like this and emptied!"' (5.13). This is followed by a communal Amen. The effect of this social engineering is rather sullied by the typical final word from Nehemiah to God in the chapter: 'God remember me favourably for all that I have done for this people!'

Chapter 7 is the fulcrum of the book. Here the first-person sections end, and there is a list of returnees, comparable with that in Ezra 2. From then on, the book is about Ezra, rather than Nehemiah. In chapter 8 he and his colleagues lead the people through instruction in the Torah in a way which has clear application to the circumstances of the people. ('They read from the book of the law of God clearly, made its sense plain, and gave instruction in what was read' (8.8).) This account suggests two things. First, that there was an identifiable corpus of Torah available to read. And second it suggests a model for the religious nurture of future generations of Jews who would be the people of the book. And then in chapter 9 there is a confession of sin by the people which represents the final act in the ending of defilement, making covenant once again possible. This time the Covenant is witnessed specifically by 'our princes, our Levites, and our priests' (9.38). There is particular emphasis in the covenant agreement, spelled out in chapter 10, on refraining from mixed marriage, keeping the sabbath, and maintaining the life of the temple and its personnel. The remaining chapters read like assorted appendices.

The material in these books has been largely dismissed by Christian readers, who see little more than a descent into a narrow legalism. Feminist critics make much of the ban on mixed marriages and the break-up of existing marriages, pointing out the disproportionate effect on women. But from a more social or anthropological viewpoint, what the books describe is the efforts of a group under threat to maintain identity, or re-brand, in a way that is both sustainable and yet faithful to the received tradition. Israel enters the Exile as a holy nation. It emerges from these post-exilic books as a holy people, a holy community, a holy minority perhaps even among Jews.

CHAPTER 18 SUMMARY

What is this chapter about?

This chapter looks at Old Testament material so far not covered. There is discussion of the contents of Jonah, Ruth, Esther, Ecclesiastes, Lamentations and Song of Songs.

What books are referred to?

The only new book referred to is Athalya Brenner, *A Feminist Companion to the Song of Songs* (Sheffield: JSOT Press, 2000).

What other books would be helpful?

A very readable approach to Song of Songs is Carey Ellen Walsh, *Exquisite Desire: Religion, the Erotic and Song of Songs* (Minneapolis: Fortress Press, 2000). Otherwise find the most recent commentaries from authors you have learned to trust.

How is the chapter organized?

Each of the books mentioned above is described in turn.

What should I be able to do by the end of this chapter?

Recognize the books in question and be able to recount their provenance.

Describe the contents of the books.

Relate the material contained therein to other Old Testament writings.

18

Five Scrolls and a Prophet

In order to complete our survey of Old Testament literature there are five further books which we must consider, together with one book, counted among the twelve minor prophets, which is more appropriately treated with this group. The prophet is Jonah, and the five books form a group called the Megilloth or Scrolls. Different versions of the Bible, ancient and modern, Hebrew and English place these scroll writings in different places among the canon. What they have in common is that each of them is designated to be read at a particular Jewish festival – a custom that continues to this day.

Jonah is unique among the books of prophets in that its contents are expressed completely in the form of narrative. It is a story about a prophet, rather than a series of oracles. The book is normally dated in the Persian period and is sometimes seen as a reaction to the very religious policies of Ezra and Nehemiah that we saw in the last chapter. For the message of this book is that Israel must be true to a God of all peoples and not indulge in any kind of xenophobia. The early part of the story is well known. Jonah is sent by God to prophesy to Nineveh, a task he tries unsuccessfully to avoid. The message to Nineveh is that it must repent of its wickedness. Nineveh was the capital of Assyria, one-time power in the region, but no longer. Eventually Jonah delivers his message to these hated foreign enemies. Against all the odds they do in fact repent. Jonah is unwilling to accept that God's grace might then be extended to them. There are some textual points of interest – the provenance of the poem in chapter 2 for example – but most of the interest lies in the theological content of the book.

If we think of this work as post-exilic, we must consider it in connection with the new kinds of theological awareness we have already noted, one of which is the awareness that God is God of the whole world. The implication of this is not just that God has power and influence over the world but that he can be universally consistent in his gracious offer of forgiveness and love. This claim will always be seen as controversial to some extent by those, Jews or Christians, who believe that they have a special relationship with God. The first part of Jonah reaffirms God's universal sovereignty over the elements and creation generally. This leads to the more controversial claims about God's universal concern. This is the context in which to read the book, rather than to see it as a direct response to the edicts of Ezra and Nehemiah about racial purity, though they do act as a particular example of what is at stake. It is worth noting that Jonah and these books are mutually exclusive in their views about God; and that itself is interesting as we consider what kind of work the Old Testament as a whole actually is, and how it is to be read. The sub-text of the book is that just as Israel has accepted God's forgiveness and entered a new phase of their lives after the Exile, so also that opportunity must be offered to others. In this respect, 'Nineveh' can stand for any alien power group. This book is realistic in that it leaves the issue unresolved, with Jonah simply sulking, disappointed with God's response to Nineveh's repentance. It is also properly designated 'prophetic' in that the message it delivers is a direct challenge to Israel's own thinking and behaviour, setting the nature of God and its implications at odds with Israel's own presentation of him in their religious life.

Reflection on text

Read Jonah 3.1—4.4. This is a key passage in the book and sets out the dilemma. Having read the passage do you think it would be fair to say that its theme is along the lines of: 'It's OK to pay lip-service to a view of God, but the practical implications of that may mean crossing boundaries you are not willing to cross?' Can you think of modern applications for this dilemma? How satisfying do you find the conclusion to it all in the following chapter?

This could also be said to be the theme of the book of **Ruth**. Although one of the Writings, and dating from post-exilic times, it is usually placed in Christian Bibles in the middle of the Former Prophets, between Judges and 1 Samuel. This is probably to try and locate it in the developing historical narrative, since it describes a time three generations before King David. But its thrust has nothing to do with history and everything to do with attitudes towards foreigners. Ruth is a Moabitess, hardly more popular than the people of Nineveh. According to Deuteronomy 23.3f., 'No Ammonite or Moabite, even down to the tenth generation, may become a member of the assembly of the Lord. They must never become members of the assembly of the Lord because they did not meet you with food and water on your journey from Egypt . . .' However, Ruth's story is one of submission and generosity. Having married an Israelite and become one of the family with all its religious obligations, her husband dies, and she is urged by her mother-in-law to return to her own people, but she refuses. 'Do not urge me to go back and desert you. Where you go, I shall go, and where you stay I shall stay. Your people will be my people, and your God, my God' (Ruth 1.16). It is as a result of this decision that she is enabled to maintain the male line that will eventually lead, three generations later, to David himself. The story may be compared to that of Judah and Tamar in Genesis 38, which also recounts heroic resistance by a woman, and the maintenance of the male line. The controversial and challenging conclusion of the book is that even David had foreign blood in his veins. This too may be seen as a pertinent message for the times of Ezra and Nehemiah.

However, in more recent scholarship, more attention has been paid to the narrative art of the author, and to the relationships described in the story itself. Here we see an artfully creative exploration of the relationship between the sexes and between power and weakness. To take just one example: the gender roles are reversed from the traditional presentation in Genesis 2.24, where a man is told to leave his parents and cling to his wife. Here Ruth does not leave her mother-in-law but clings to her (same verb). God is frequently mentioned but is not really a player in the drama, and it has been pointed out that this *is* essentially a drama in six scenes which consist mainly of dialogue. Feminist critics have found much to reflect on in this story, and it is likely that future work on this book will follow their lead. Ruth has an established place in the tradition (as evidenced in Matthew 1.5). The link-age of the book to the feast of Weeks, a harvest festival, is coincidental and probably derives from the later action of the book being set at the time of the barley harvest.

The third enigmatic 'novel' or extended narrative, and one which also has a heroine, is the book of **Esther**. The setting of this book is the Persian empire, and its Jewish characters are those, the great majority, who have opted to remain in the 'foreign' land rather than return to Jerusalem with Nehemiah. The issue with which the book deals is the precarious situation of those who want to maintain their identity as Jews when they are living outside their own land. It therefore has many modern applications. The story concerns a plot against the Jews, which Esther foils and, more than that, manages to turn against the plotter, so that he is killed and they gain power. Again, it is a well told story, a good read, and one of the funniest in the Old Testament. Chapters 6 and 7 read like a scene from a modern farce, with a climax full of misunderstanding and double-meaning, when the chief plotter, Haman, throws himself at Queen Esther to beg for mercy, and the king thinks he is trying to assault her! He is then hanged on the very gallows he had had erected to hang Mordecai the Jew. But that very humour is part of the author's art, in that it is consciously juxtaposed with an horrific story about attempted genocide. Christians have sometimes struggled to discern 'scripture' in this story, which appears to glory in the downfall of Israel's enemies. Of particular concern is the fact that, alone of all the books in the Bible, this one never mentions God. Rabbinic Judaism interprets this absence in a positive way, as do some Christian authors, along the lines of God's providence being obvious without necessity for mention by name. God is, in other words, hidden. In Hebrew the word *astir* (very similar to Esther, in Hebrew) means 'I will hide.' Other verses lend themselves to this kind of interpretation. The first letters of the Hebrew words in 5.4 ('Let the king and Haman come today') are Y,H,W,H, for example. God is, in other words, 'hiding in the text'. Esther is best read through at one sitting. It is read today at the Jewish festival of Purim (meaning lots), in a way which highlights the comic, in that readers compete to see who can read it fastest. That too has a dark side, as in this case the nationalistic triumphalism is celebrated with humour and carnival. Esther is the most unashamedly

Jewish statement in the canon. It may be compared with other 'novels' such as the early chapters of Daniel or the story of Joseph, both of which describe precarious life, but ultimate triumph, for Jews in diaspora situations.

The book of **Qoheleth** or **Ecclesiastes** has also struggled to be regarded as scripture by both Jews and Christians. It appears to be at odds with much traditional teaching, and even goes beyond the bounds of subversion that Job illustrates. Modern agnostics would find little to disagree with in the book. It may be that its ascription to Solomon rescued it, in the eyes of rabbinic Jews. Nevertheless, that was some concession, because it appears to deny life after death, which was an important belief for Pharisees. Its standpoint, in fact, is precisely an observation on life made in the sure knowledge that we shall die. This book's form is similar to that of Proverbs, that is, an anthology style, and there is some debate about how the collection came into being and how many authors were involved. The apocryphal book Ecclesiasticus is a response to this book, which is usually dated around 250 BCE. There is ample mention of God here, but in a very philosophical determinist mode, without the usual religious commentary making links between humankind and God either through God's intervention in human affairs or through human ritual in worship and prayer. God is remote and there is no evidence of his interest. This scroll is read during the autumn harvest festival of booths, for no obvious reason. The injunctions toward enjoying yourself may explain it, or it may be that the cynical, time-worn author's mood matches autumn. This is not a book to read if you're having a bad hair day.

At first sight that is also true of **Lamentations**. This scroll is read at the solemn commemoration of the destruction of the temple, on the ninth of Ab. It is a series of five very formal poems, which take the reader through an experience of bereavement. The 'death' in this case is the sacking of Jerusalem immediately prior to the Exile to Babylon as described at 2 Kings 25.8ff. It is not too much to describe this in terms of a bereavement, as the poems themselves personify Jerusalem as a woman. We have already seen how central a part these early years of the Exile play in the development of Old Testament theology. Everything the faithful thought they knew about God was called into question. The inconceivable had happened. Lamentations starts with the word, 'How?' (*Ekah?*) and that is its name in the Hebrew scriptures. How could God allow this to happen? How can the faithful understand the way of God in these events? How is faith going to be possible in the future? These are the post-traumatic questions with which the book deals, and which will touch a chord with the traumatized in every generation.

Reflection on text

Read Lamentations 3.25–66. This passage gives a sense of the whole, and some commentators find it central to understanding the book. Note particularly the changing moods of hope and despair. Compare them with what was said about the lament form of psalm in Chapter 16. How 'realistic' do you find this kind of expression? How important is it to be able to place it historically?

The English name, 'Lamentations', reflects the fact that each of the five poems contained in the work conforms to the genre 'lament'. Gunkel's work on the Psalms identified this as the most important form in the Psalms, and subsequent work by Westermann and others has confirmed that view and analysed the form further. The laments in Lamentations have a very strict pattern. Four of the five are acrostics. That is each line or, in the case of the third poem, each series of lines, begins with successive letters of the Hebrew alphabet. (So the first line begins with aleph, the second with beth, the third with gimel, etc.) The fifth poem is not arranged in this way but has 22 lines: the number of letters in the Hebrew alphabet. Such an arrangement is not uncommon in Hebrew poetry. For example Psalm 119 has 22 stanzas, and each line of any particular stanza begins with the same (again successive) letter of the alphabet. It may be that this is an aid to memory. It may be a way of symbolizing completeness (the absolute A to Z). It may be associated with a form of devotion (perhaps like the modern rosary) that involves a degree of repetition alongside successive movement. The poems show another common feature of Hebrew poetry in that they are 'chiastic'. That is, for example, in a pattern of five (as here with five chapters), number 1 and number 5 will reflect each other, as will 2 and 4, and 3 will be the core of the work. This pattern can be seen both in the arrangement of the chapters, and internally within each poem. None of which is to say that all the poems derive from the same hand. It is assumed that the poems were written soon after the events they reflect upon. Their intensity seems to demand that, but authorship is unknown. The link with Jeremiah is in terms of content, rather than any other historical ascription.

Following the clues set by the chiastic structure would lead us to think that the core of meaning in the book might be found in the central part of chapter 3, and many scholars would agree. Here we find the only note of hope in the book, and the only connection between present experience and the pre-Exile hope. Precisely because of that other scholars have been cautious to read, for example, 3.21–36 as if it somehow annulled the reality of grief and loss. However, it is not necessary to read the verses in that way. The psalm laments commonly contain messages of hope in the midst of suffering, and they reflect the experience of those who hope against hope in such situations. Easter Day does not simply annul Good Friday in the Christian tradition. They stand side by side. And so it is here that the truthful, honest sadness and bereavement are accompanied by brief glimpses of hope that make life bearable and faith possible. There is something very contemporary about this brief but valuable book.

But the scroll which remains exemplifies, perhaps best of all, what has been happening in biblical scholarship these past years, and that is **Song of Songs** (a Hebrew idiom, meaning 'The Best Song'). This scroll is read at the celebration of Passover. Essentially, it is a series of erotic love poems in which four voices are heard: a female, a male, a female chorus and a male chorus. Historical criticism was interested in its date and origin. It has some interesting linguistic features that, among other things, suggest a post-Persian period for the final redaction. But how did the text reach that stage? Are the poems an anthology, or are they in sequence? Are there other literary forms in the ancient world (such as the Arabic *wasf*, for example) with which it might be compared? Are there links with other biblical writings that use male and female imagery extensively, such as Hosea? Is the writer reviving the imagery of the garden of Eden? Does it have a theme, or any editorial unity? Alongside these questions was interest in how the book made it into the canon at all. Its subject matter, after all, is quite unusual in the Bible, and some kind of allegorical answer seemed to be called for to justify its inclusion. So this was not just about two lovers. It was about God and Israel, or

Jesus and the church. And even if that seemed unconvincing, at least it was about a man and wife. So, for example, Schofield: 'The experience of human love between bride and bridegroom, husband and wife, can open human life to an appreciation and understanding of the intensity of God's love, and the bliss of seeking and finding him' (Schofield 1969, p. 325).

Recently, however, criticism has taken new directions. Many of the historical approaches have been seen as largely irrelevant, and allegorical interpretations as being unnecessary – albeit that scholars accept that such interpretation probably was responsible for its inclusion in the writings after debate at the Council of Jamnia. It is not necessarily about marriage. Critics such as Brenner believe the love described is of an erotic non-marital kind. Sexual consummation is certainly in view, however. Following these radical thoughts is the suggestion that the author may be female. There is a matriarchal emphasis throughout. The sexual fantasy of the female is said to be recognizably genuine. There is reference to 'my mother's house' (3.4; 8.2). There is also a marked lack of sexism, and a predominant role for the female. Those who oppose the allegorical reading point to it being forced and difficult to sustain with two characters. There is a wealth of detail, which does not lend itself to such interpretation, and the piece does seem to have a single continuous plot. These scholars, predominantly female, believe that the book should be taken at face value.

Reflection on text

Read Song of Songs 5.2–8. This is said to be one of the more obviously erotic fantasies of the woman. If you are a woman you might like to consider how authentic such a passage feels. If you are a man you may prefer to read 4.1–12 and consider whether you think a man or a woman might have written this.

From a different perspective, but equally dissatisfied with the interpretations of the past, David Clines thinks the book is a piece of ancient pornography – a fantastic piece of wish-fulfilment by a male who gets a kick out of trying to imagine how women think about sex. In the process he believes the book demeans women. Other women writers believe it to be the exact opposite – rather a consecration of human sexual love – and that we access this true message only if we embrace the whole text as it stands. In my own teaching I tend to begin courses on the Old Testament with Song of Songs. This has the effect of introducing young students to something they recognize and are interested in, and that interest helps them to puzzle, and to ask the questions that critics through the centuries have been asking about this collection of books. And from the start it helps them to recognize themselves as readers who have been affected by what they read. The reality is, as it has always been, outside the narrow academic community, that people do not read the Old Testament to find out more about ancient culture. They read it to find out more about themselves, about life's purpose and destiny and about how to behave and what makes it worth it.

19

Work in Progress

Anyone having reached this point and who is expecting that this final chapter is going to list the assured results of scholarship on the Old Testament in some easily memorable form, is in for a disappointment. Although, having said that, few who have actually read and worked their way through the book would expect that anyway. The fact is that at this time, the only assured result of scholarship is that all results throughout the past two thousand years have proved to be provisional. There was a time around the middle of the twentieth century when scholars were dangerously close to an agreement on what there was to know about the Old Testament, but that time has given way to a present in which even the most fundamental issues, such as, how to read the Old Testament, are disputed. And so it is more appropriate, at the end of the book, to summarize the areas where there is disagreement and where work continues.

One main area of dispute is that about which set of critical tools might be used to unlock the Old Testament to modern readers. The choice of the last two hundred years or so has been the tools of the historian. This has directed scholars towards finding out more about the origins of the biblical text, and the context in which that text was transmitted and developed into its final form. It has also presupposed discrimination in favour of seeing the texts as in some way disclosing historical information. The test of truth for what the texts contained was thereby tied up with questions about what happened and how we can know. Questions for debate in the faith community and elsewhere included those about how supernatural material (seas being parted, or God speaking to people in gardens, having created the world in seven days) or abnormal material (people living to ages well in excess of what we now expect) was to be treated. Historical archaeological evidence was in some cases sought to support points of view.

The more recent choice has been to attempt to unlock the Old Testament using the critical tools used by scholars of literature. Understandably this has been treated with caution in some quarters because it completely redefines the kind of truth that the texts might contain. 'What happened' is no longer anything like as important as why the author wrote in a particular way; what tools s/he uses to persuade us of a particular point of view; what effect the writing has on me, and what I bring to the text in a way that affects my understanding of it. So we have seen a movement from treating the texts as reliable accounts of what happened, with accompanying commentary from a YHWH faith perspective; to treating the texts as something like serious historical novels and dramas that are profound and meant to raise fundamental questions for us in the way that all serious art does, but written from a particular faith perspective.

This has led to a change in the way that Old Testament texts are described. For two hundred years this description has taken the form of *exegesis* – attempting to read out from the text all the information that it contains, together with whatever supporting material about its origins will enable us to access its meaning to the first readers or hearers. Now commentaries are more concerned with the narrative art of writers or their rhetorical strategy. Attempts to access the meanings which the text contains are more likely *eisegetical*, that is, reading into the text from the reader's own situation in a way that will enable connections to be made between text and experience. As such they are no longer *definitive*, relying on the accumulation of expertise for their authority, but rather *suggestive*, helping the reader to make their own connections and see what the text might mean for them, in a way that makes authenticity more important than authority. The kinds of new commentary that this task demands are beginning to appear, and it seems certain that this task will continue in the foreseeable future.

Connected with the move toward literary methods of criticism is a new appreciation of the Old Testament as a part of the canon of Christian scripture. This means taking a new interest in the arrangement and re-arrangement of the books, and perhaps also their relationship with the New Testament. At a more fundamental level, though, it means accepting that the

Old Testament is to some degree a crafted and designed faith-community (which is to say, human) creation, in a way that scholars have been loath to do in the past. Those who have been inspired by Brevard Childs's books on canonical criticism are among the most prolific writers at present, and even those who disagree with his conclusions use some of his terminology to articulate their own approaches.

It is not very long since some scholars thought that sociology was the discipline most likely to take Old Testament studies forward, and certainly sociology has made and continues to make a valuable contribution from a number of directions. It is this discipline that has led to a new assessment of the motives of writers, and to the kind of analysis of texts that is interested in how power is exercised through the text. It is this discipline also which has been responsible for one of the most influential contributions to the question about the origins of Israel – Norman Gottwald's *Tribes of Yahweh* (1979). Social description is likely to play a large part in the continuing debate about the relationship between the actual history of the 1500 years or so before the common era, and the biblical accounts. For even if we accept the most extreme of the literary theses, questions still remain about why and in what context the texts were written, preserved and used. This 'new historical quest' has a long way to run, and, I suspect, there is still much to be discovered under the auspices of the old quest, which will be useful in the new.

However, it is also true that attention is shifting away from the supposed period of the Exodus, Settlement and monarchy, and toward the (supposed) period of the Exile. Inevitably this will lead to some shift in the interest of scholars. At the moment, for example, there is far more to be read in English about the Deuteronomistic history than there is about that of 1 and 2 Chronicles. I suspect that in the future that balance will be redressed and we shall see more works concentrating on what have until now been fairly unfashionable areas of research.

Apart from the debates about history and appropriate commentary, the new reading approaches have led to reassessment in thematic studies. The most obvious example is the field of Old Testament ethics. Until relatively recently, descriptions of Old Testament ethics have followed a three-stage historical process which has been relatively unaware of the critical debates about hermeneutics. In this process, stage one would be represented by discussion of the Ten Commandments and accompanying material. Stage two would concentrate on the ethical content of the prophets' teaching about personal responsibility. Stage three would chart the descent into legalism represented in post-exilic writings. In fact, this has not been a popular field of study for obvious reasons. Apart from these three sorts of material, how could anyone seriously claim that the Old Testament is, in any sense, an appropriate source for ethical teaching? Many of its stories apparently applaud behaviour, both personal and civic, that we would find offensive or difficult to defend. Its laws appear draconian, giving, for example, the power of life and death to parents with regard to their children. And some Christians might want to argue that one of the merits of the New Testament teaching of Jesus is that it offered an alternative to the kind of legalism into which Old Testament ethics allegedly descended.

During the past ten years, however, and more frequently recently, there has been more writing in this area, which does take account of the insights of recent scholarship. C. J. H. Wright's *Living as the People of God: The Relevance of Old Testament Ethics* (1983) could be regarded as the first contribution to the modern debate (it has now been revised and combined with his *Walking in the Ways of the Lord* (1995) in *Old Testament Ethics for the People of God* (2004)), but John Barton's John Albert Hall Lectures, *Ethics and the Old Testament* (1998) are probably the best place to start. He believes that the key to accessing Old Testament ethics is realizing that it is the stories, the narrative materials, which contain the enduring ethical material rather than the codes. Mary Mills builds on this insight in her more substantial *Biblical Morality: Moral Perspectives in Old Testament Narratives* (2001). She sets out a framework for reading narrative from an ethical perspective in terms of a threefold or three-level approach. This sees the human person as a moral agent essentially set in a social context which has a yet wider context of significance and destiny. So her three categories are person, community and cosmos. The person category is related to character in the narrative; the community aspect to plot, and the category of cosmos to narratives such as Genesis 1—11, the apocalyptic portions of Daniel and the book of Job. Alongside this, mention might be made of Cyril Rodd's *Glimpses of a Strange Land: Studies in Old Testament Ethics* (2001), which maintains the strangeness and in a sense, inaccessibility, of the world in which anything which might be described as 'ethics' is set out in the Old Testament. He reacts against any attempt to systematize Old Testament ethics, or to avoid the many awkward questions that still remain even with the new freedom granted the reader by modern critics. This is one example of a field of study that could be said to be in its infancy.

This is an exciting time to be studying the Old Testament. The anorak-clad world of lists of kings, sets of laws, the possible routes of the Exodus, types of psalms, varieties of ritual and the results of ancient wars has given way to a more stylishly dressed world of power struggles, sex, glamour, celebrity, ideological battles, politics and observation of the human condition which seems both more recognizable and more interesting. Time will tell to what extent, and how quickly, the communities of faith whose life is both nurtured and defined by these ancient texts will take to the makeover.

References

Achtemeier, E. (1986), *Nahum–Malachi*, Atlanta: John Knox Press

Adam, A. K. M. (1995), *What is Post Modern Biblical Criticism?* Minneapolis: Fortress Press

Albright, W. (1939), 'The Israelite conquest in the light of archaeology', *Bulletin of the American Schools of Oriental Research* 74, pp. 11–22

Alt, A. (1968), 'The settlement of the Israelites in Palestine', in R. Wilson (trans.), *Essays on Old Testament History and Religion*, Garden City NY: Doubleday

Alter, R. (1998), 'The poetic and wisdom books', in J. Barton (ed.), *The Cambridge Companion to Biblical Interpretation*, Cambridge: Cambridge University Press

Anderson, B. W. (1994), *From Creation to New Creation: Old Testament Perspectives*, Minneapolis: Fortress Press

Auld, A. G. (1989), 'Prophecy and the prophets', in S. Bigger (ed.), *Creating the Old Testament*, Oxford: Blackwell

Baker, D., and B. Arnold (eds) (1999), *The Face of Old Testament Studies*, Leicester: IVP

Balentine, S. E. (2002), *Leviticus*, Louisville: Westminster John Knox Press

Barr, J. (1999), *The Concept of Biblical Theology: An Old Testament Perspective*, London: SCM Press

Barton, J. (1984), *Reading the Old Testament*, London: Darton, Longman & Todd

Barton, J. (1997), *Making the Christian Bible*, London: Darton, Longman & Todd

Barton, J. (1998), *Ethics and the Old Testament*, London: SCM Press

Barton, J. (ed.) (1998), *The Cambridge Companion to Biblical Interpretation*, Cambridge: Cambridge University Press

Bible and Culture Collective (1995), *The Postmodern Bible*, New Haven: Yale University Press

Brenner, A. (2000), *A Feminist Companion to the Song of Songs*, Sheffield: JSOT Press

Brown, M. J. (2000), *What They Don't Tell You: A Survivor's Guide to Biblical Studies*, Louisville: John Knox Press

Brueggemann, W. (1982), *Genesis*, Atlanta: John Knox Press

Brueggemann, W. (1984), *The Message of the Psalms: A Theological Commentary*, Minneapolis: Augsburg

Brueggemann, W. (1991), 'Bounded by obedience and praise: the Psalms as canon', *Journal for the Study of the Old Testament* 50, pp. 63–92

Brueggemann, W. (1992), *Old Testament Theology: Essays on Structure, Theme and Text*, ed. Patrick D. Miller, Minneapolis: Fortress Press

Brueggemann, W. (1997), *Cadences of Home*, Louisville: Westminster John Knox Press

Brueggemann, W. (2001), *Deuteronomy*, Nashville: Abingdon

Brueggemann, W. (2003), *An Introduction to the Old Testament: The Canon and Christian Imagination*, London: Westminster John Knox Press

Carter, C. E. (2001), 'Social scientific approaches', in L. G. Perdue (ed.), *The Blackwell Companion to the Hebrew Bible*, Oxford: Blackwell, pp. 36–53

Ceresko, A. (1992), *Introduction to the Old Testament: A Liberation Perspective*, London: Geoffrey Chapman

Childs, B. S. (1970), *Biblical Theology in Crisis*, Philadelphia: Westminster

Childs, B. S. (1974), *Exodus*, London: SCM Press

Childs, B. S. (1979), *Introduction to the Old Testament as Scripture*, London: SCM Press

Childs, B. S. (1985), *Old Testament Theology in a Canonical Context*, London: SCM Press

Childs, B. S. (1992), *Biblical Theology of the Old and New Testaments*, London: SCM Press

Clements, R. E. (1968), *God's Chosen People*, London: SCM Press

Clements, R. E. (1976), *A Century of Old Testament Study*, London: Lutterworth

Clements, R. E. (1997), *Deuteronomy*, 2nd edn Sheffield: JSOT Press

Clines, D. (1979/1996), *The Theme of the Pentateuch*, Sheffield: Sheffield Academic Press

Clines, D. (1989, 2000, 2005), *Job* (3 vols), Waco, Texas: Word Commentaries

Clines, D. (1995), *Interested Parties*, Sheffield: Sheffield Academic Press

Coggins, R. (1990), *Introducing the Old Testament*, Oxford: Oxford University Press

Cone, J. (1977), *God of the Oppressed*, London: SPCK

Cross, F. M. (1973), *Canaanite Myth and Hebrew Epic: Essays in the History and Religion of Israel*, Cambridge, Mass.: Harvard University Press

Davies, P. R. (1992), *In Search of Ancient Israel*, Sheffield: JSOT Press

Dempster, S. (2001), *Dominion and Dynasty*, Leicester: IVP

Dever, W. G. (2001), *What Did the Biblical Writers Know and When Did They Know It?*, Grand Rapids, Mich.: Eerdmans

Dever, W. G. (2003), *Who Were the Early Israelites and Where Did They Come From?*, Grand Rapids, Mich.: Eerdmans

Eaton, J. H. (1987), *Job*, Sheffield: JSOT Press

Eichrodt, W. (1961, 1967), *Theology of the Old Testament* (2 vols), trans. J. A. Baker, Philadelphia: Westminster Press

Finkelstein, I. (1988), *The Archaeology of Israelite Settlement*, Jerusalem: Israel Explanation Society

Fritz, V. (1994), *An Introduction to Biblical Archaeology*, Sheffield: JSOT Press

Gerstenberger, E. (2002), *Theologies in the Old Testament*, Edinburgh: T & T Clark

Gooder, P. (2000), *The Pentateuch: A Story of Beginnings*, London: Continuum

Gottwald, N. (1979), *The Tribes of Yahweh*, London: SCM Press

Gottwald, N. and R. Horsley (eds) (1993), *The Bible and Liberation*, London: SPCK

Gowan, D. (2000), *Eschatology in the Old Testament*, Edinburgh: T & T Clark

Gowan, D. (2001), *Daniel*, Nashville: Abingdon Press

Goulder, M. (1998), *The Psalms of the Return*, Book Five *Pss 107–150*, Sheffield: Sheffield Academic Press

Gunn, D. and D. Fewell (1993), *Narrative in the Hebrew Bible*, Oxford: Oxford University Press

Heaton, E. W. (1996), *A Short Introduction to the Old Testament Prophets*, 2nd edn, Oxford: Oneworld

Holdsworth, J. (2003), *Dwelling in a Strange Land: Exile in the Bible and in the Church*, Norwich: Canterbury Press

Kirsch, J. (1997), *The Harlot by the Side of the Road: Forbidden Tales of the Bible*, London: Rider

Klein, R. (2001), 'Narrative texts: Chronicles, Ezra and Nehemiah', in L. G. Perdue (ed.), *The Blackwell Companion to the Hebrew Bible*, Oxford: Blackwell, pp. 385–401

Lohfink, N. (1994), *Theology of the Pentateuch*, Edinburgh: T & T Clark

McDermott, J. J. (1998), *What Are They Saying about the Formation of Israel?*, New York: Paulist Press

Mason, R. (1997), *Propaganda and Subversion in the Old Testament*, London: SPCK

Mendenhall, G. E. (1955), *Law and Covenant in Israel and the Ancient Near East*, Pittsburgh: Biblical Colloquium

Mendenhall, G. E. (1962), 'The Hebrew conquest of Palestine', *Biblical Archaeologist* 25/3, pp. 66–87

Mendenhall, G. E. (2001), *Ancient Israel's Faith and History*, London: Wesminster John Knox Press

Meyers, C. (2001), 'Early Israel and the rise of the Israelite monarchy', in L. G. Perdue (ed.), *The Blackwell Companion to the Hebrew Bible*, Oxford: Blackwell, pp. 61–86

Miller, P. D. (1990), *Deuteronomy*, Louisville: John Knox Press

Miller, P. D. (2000), *Israelite Religion and Biblical Theology: Collected Essays*, Sheffield: Sheffield Academic Press

Mills, M. (1999), *Historical Israel: Biblical Israel*, London: Cassell

Mills, M. (2001), *Biblical Morality: Moral Perspectives in Old Testament Narratives*, Aldershot: Ashgate

Noth, M. (1960), *The History of Israel*, London: Blackwell

Oestreicher, P. (1986), *The Double Cross*, London: Darton, Longman & Todd

Perdue, L. G. (ed.) (2001), *The Blackwell Companion to the Hebrew Bible*, Oxford: Blackwell

Pleins, J. D. (1993), *The Psalms: Songs of Tragedy, Hope, and Justice*, Maryknoll, NY: Orbis Books

Powell, M. A. (1993), *What is Narrative Criticism?*, London: SPCK

Rendtorff, R. (1985), *The Old Testament: An Introduction*, London: SCM Press

Richards, H. J. (1973), *The First Christmas: What Really Happened?*, London: Fontana

Richards, H. J. (1976), *The First Easter: What Really Happened?*, London: Fontana

Robinson, T. H. (1923/1953), *Prophecy and the Prophets in Ancient Israel*, London: Duckworth

Rogerson, J. (ed.) (1983), *Beginning Old Testament Study*, London: SPCK

Russell, D. S. (1964), *The Method and Message of Jewish Apocalyptic*, London: SCM Press

Russell, D. S. (1992), *Divine Disclosure*, London: SCM Press

Rodd, C. S. (2001), *Glimpses of a Strange Land: Studies in Old Testament Ethics*, Edinburgh: T & T Clark

Sawyer, J. F. A. (1993), *Prophecy and the Biblical Prophets*, 2nd end, Oxford: Oxford University Press

Schofield, J. N. (1969), *Law, Prophets and Writings*, London: SPCK

Soggin, J. A. (1976), *Introduction to the Old Testament*, London: SCM Press

Stewart, D. (2001), *Exegesis: A Handbook for Students and Pastors*, 3rd edn, Louisville: Westminster John Knox Press

Van Wolde, E. (1997), *Mr and Mrs Job*, London: SCM Press

Von Rad, G. (1962/5), *Old Testament Theology* (2 vols), London: SCM Press

Von Rad, G. (1966), *Deuteronomy*, London: SCM Press

Walsh, C. (2000), *Exquisite Desire: Religion, the Erotic and Song of Songs*, Minneapolis: Fortress Press

Wenham, G. (1999), 'Pondering the Pentateuch', in D. Baker and B. Arnold (eds), *The Face of Old Testament Studies*, Leicester: IVP

Westermann, C. (1969), *Handbook to the Old Testament*, London: SPCK

Whitelam, K. (1996), *The Invention of Ancient Israel*, London: Routledge

Williamson, H. G. M. (1982), *1 and 2 Chronicles*, Grand Rapids, Mich.: Eerdmans

Wilson, G. H. (1985), *The Editing of the Hebrew Psalter*, Chico, Calif.: Scholars Press

Whybray, N. (1998), *Job*, Sheffield: Sheffield Academic Press

Wright, C. J. H. (1983), *Living as the People of God: The Relevance of Old Testament Ethics*, Leicester: IVP

Wright, C. J. H. (1995), *Walking in the Ways of the Lord*, Leicester: Apollos

Wright, C. J. H. (2004), *Old Testament Ethics for the People of God*, Leicester: IVP

Index of Biblical References